The Arts & Crafts Houses
OF MASSACHUSETTS

 W9-BMM-985

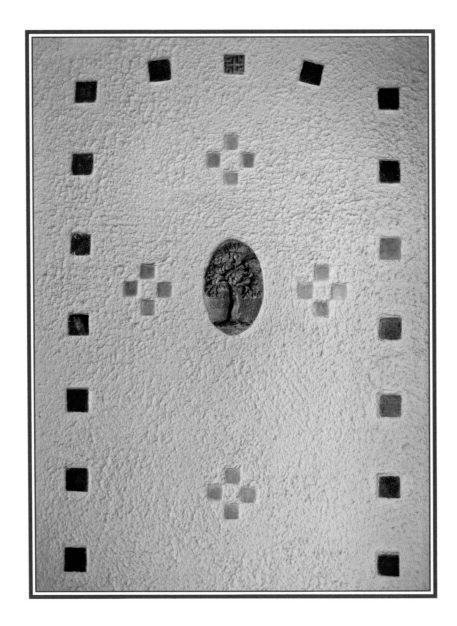

The Arts & Crafts Houses

OF MASSACHUSETTS

A STYLE REDISCOVERED

HELI MELTSNER

Bauhan Publishing ✦ Peterborough, New Hampshire ✦ 2019

©2019 Heli Meltsner   All Rights Reserved
ISBN: 978-0-87233-273-7

Library of Congress Cataloging-in-Publication Data
Names: Meltsner, Heli, author.
Title: The arts and crafts houses of Massachusetts : a style rediscovered / Heli Meltsner.
Description: Peterborough, NH : Bauhan Publishing, 2019. | Includes bibliographical references.
Identifiers: LCCN 2019014404 | ISBN 9780872332737 (softcover : alk. paper)
Subjects: LCSH: Architecture, Domestic—Massachusetts—History--20th century. | Arts and crafts movement—Massachusetts. | Architecture, Domestic--Massachusetts--History—20th century—Guidebooks. | Arts and crafts movement—Massachusetts—Guidebooks.
Classification: LCC NA7235.M4 M45 2019 | DDC 720.9744/09041--dc23
LC record available at https://lccn.loc.gov/2019014404

Book design by Henry James and Sarah Bauhan
Cover design by Henry James
Front cover photograph of 1547 Centre Street, Newton, Massachusetts by Heli Meltsner
Frontispiece photograph of 219 Buckminster Road in Brookline, Massachusetts by Heli Meltsner

PO BOX 117 PETERBOROUGH NEW HAMPSHIRE 03458

WWW.BAUHANPUBLISHING.COM   Printed in the United States of America

For Lucy, Anna, Will, and Tessa

CONTENTS

INTRODUCTION

As an architectural historian, I have for years explored and documented the communities of Massachusetts, looking with a passionate and professional gaze at their domestic architecture. During my travels I became fascinated by a group of early twentieth century Arts and Crafts houses documenting the state's architecture. I found that the agency responsible for preserving the state's historic architecture had overlooked the significance of these Arts and Crafts houses, and I wondered why we should we pay attention to them[1]

I am sure that these houses deserve to be studied, described and documented. As a group they are lively, and, though diverse, they are united by distinct characteristics. This book brings these underappreciated houses to the notice of architects and architectural historians, as well as others interested in domestic architecture. It also explores questions such as why the houses look as they do and how that came about. It has been my pleasure to live with these charming houses on a daily basis, and I can say that they have repaid every bit of attention I have given them.

This Arts and Crafts style is an American adaptation of the last flowering of the more well-known Arts and Crafts Movement that occurred in Britain roughly between 1890 and World War I. Massachusetts architects, craftsmen, and craftswomen enthusiastically engaged with the values

and ideas of the English movement, founding The Boston Society of Arts and Crafts in 1897, the first such society in America. The Massachusetts houses influenced by the English work of the late nineteenth and early twentieth centuries were built in a relatively short period, between 1903 and 1922, and erected primarily in city suburbs or in the quasi-suburban areas of cities undergoing development during the period.

These examples of English-inspired Arts and Crafts architecture have enriched Massachusetts city streets and suburban roads for nearly a century but, like other discoveries hiding in plain sight, I believe they now require a fresh and informed eye to see them as a discrete stylistic group. Upon investigation, I discovered that contemporary architectural historians of early twentieth century Arts and Crafts work have been primarily concerned with ecclesiastical and public buildings, looking only briefly at this domestic group, although they have often suggested they merited further study and would repay thoughtful attention. Almost a quarter-century ago, the distinguished scholar Margaret Henderson Floyd wrote, "The size and importance of the Boston Society of Arts & Crafts and its relationship to architecture has only recently been recognized and remains to be fully explored. That its most influential founders were architects . . . has been documented, but the effect of this exchange on the design of buildings in Boston (or in comparison to contemporaneous developments in Chicago) has not yet been considered in detail."[2] This statement is still true for domestic architecture.

The group of Arts and Crafts houses in Massachusetts is not large but it is significant: many of the houses were designed by the state's most accomplished architects. In addition, the style was often an advance towards the modernity and simplicity that showed a path away from the contemporary historical models then in vogue. This book explores the ways America adapted English country and suburban house models to American conditions and the requirements of local owners, revealing the variety and richness of the Arts and Crafts style as it developed in Massachusetts. Looked at this way, the group makes an important contribution to our built environment.

One of the reasons this group is all but unknown is that the English version of Arts and Crafts is hard to describe, having few easily recognized physical characteristics. Even in England, these houses were not at first thought of as displaying a specific style, but as part of a movement, the collected work of architects who belonged to an Arts and Crafts Society or guild or who held roughly similar ideas about design and the importance of hand-crafted objects. And, although the Massachusetts architects designing these houses in the first two decades of the twentieth century were well known in their day, their acclaim did not long outlive them. Finally, those who practiced in the Arts and Crafts idiom also worked in a wide variety of other styles. When the Arts and Crafts approaches slipped from popularity after the end of World War I, Massachusetts architects simply abandoned them.

This is also a narrative of the unfolding of architectural history. When a new style or stylistic movement is introduced, architects themselves have few labels to attach to what they are creating. Later, historians try to fix a name to what they find to be a cohesive set of principles, architectural gestures, proportions, materials, and references to historic styles. In the case of the architecture that emerged in the eastern United States that took as a starting point the English Arts and Crafts movement, there was little to go on as the English architects themselves never achieved, nor did they wish to, a distinctive style, but rather a loose cousinship of architectural elements.

Other regions of the United States reacted to the Arts and Crafts movement in a manner that responded to their specific climates, landscapes, and popular attitudes. In northern California, architects such as Bernard Maybeck and Julia Morgan, forcefully used the medieval motifs popularized by the English architects, but with their own contemporary twist. In Pasadena, for example, between 1893 and 1914, the brothers Greene and Greene expanded the Colonial British bungalow into a spacious work of art. Highly idiosyncratic practitioners of the Arts and Crafts movement, they took its concept of showing rather than hiding both exterior and interior construction by exposing structural members, joints, and pins, all united by superb, highly finished Japanese woodworking techniques. Their practice of integrating a variety of porches, terraces, balconies, and sleeping porches directly relates to the English vision of relating the house to the garden, although without the rigid English distinction between street and garden fronts. The interiors of Greene and Greene houses are now equally famous for their remarkably smoothed and burnished built-in furniture and for their specially designed and fabricated elements such as lavish stained-glass windows, lighting fixtures, and fabrics.

Frank Lloyd Wright and the group of architects around him in Chicago made America's boldest use of the movement's reluctance to rely on historicizing forms. They too insisted on uniting the house to its site to create a dwelling that related to the wide-open spaces of the Midwest. These houses, with their broad, sheltering roofs and open plans were designed to reflect not only their region but also a new informality in living patterns. The resulting horizontality and geometric decoration of the Prairie style made the houses uncompromisingly contemporary, but they were embellished with hand-crafted stained-glass windows and elegant built-in furniture that, in a different mode, were important features of the English Arts and Crafts. In a thoroughly American manner, Wright wrote a stirring rebuttal to the anti-machine ethic of English Arts and Crafts thinkers and welcomed the machine as a democratic tool.

The only non-regional response to English Arts and Crafts movement style was created by Gustav Stickley and publicized by his *Craftsman* magazine, published between 1901 and 1916. Indeed, the first four issues of the magazine included articles on the philosophical forerunners of the English movement and by or about the seminal English Arts and Crafts architects. In 1903 the magazine began to sell homey, inexpensive house designs. A few were based on the more recognizable of the English work, but most were derived from the smaller Greene and Greene bungalows. Other plans applied Craftsman ideas and stylistic details to Mission, Prairie, New England and Dutch Colonial, and Foursquare styles or forms. The magazine also published illustrations of appropriate furniture, lighting fixtures, metal work, and do-it-yourself embroidery patterns that *Craftsman* subscribers could purchase to help them achieve both the Craftsman style and the simple, democratic, and modern lifestyle the magazine recommended.

Due to a resurgence of Craftsman style popularity in the northwestern states and among the newly proud bungalow owners, many think of the Craftsman as the sole authentic Arts and Crafts style, unaware of the America's discrete regional versions. Interest in Craftsman architecture and decoration in the last decade has been both popular and academic. The market abounds with opportunities to purchase Craftsman furniture, lighting, and hardware; periodicals and books devoted to Craftsman home design and furnishings now fill several shelves of well-stocked libraries. Websites offer everything from Craftsman custom-made doorbells to covers for hiding wall-mounted flat-screen TVs.

On the east coast, the two densest centers of English Arts and Crafts homebuilding were Massachusetts and Pennsylvania. The latter had several important conditions for responding to the English Arts and Crafts ideas about domestic architecture: plentiful local stone, a strong masonry tradition that continued well into the twentieth century, and the architect Wilson Eyre, who used native materials to great advantage in his brilliant local interpretation of English models. A small but fresh crop of architect-designed houses in this style also sprang up on Long Island and in the wealthier enclaves of New Jersey.

An authority on the prominent British Arts and Crafts architect and theorist M. H. Baillie Scott declared, "Of the great regions of architectural activity in America around 1900, the Northeast, the Midwest and California, the progressive aspect of the Arts & Crafts movement makes the least headway in the Northeast, although its influence appears to have been first felt there."[3] He is correct that in Massachusetts, architects and clients who built houses before 1900 had yet to adopt the Arts and Crafts movement, but soon afterwards they began an enthusiastic embrace, adhering more closely to English Arts and Crafts models than did other areas. Perhaps this was due to their identification with English culture and heritage. They did not fail to create a significant adaptation of the style: it was simply less visually dramatic than the western adaptations and, consequently, less well described.

Because I think that Massachusetts' experience differs from that of other areas of the country, this book chronicles the response of the state's architects to English Arts and Crafts ideas. I focus on architects because houses of this style were almost entirely designed by men who had either studied at a school of architecture or who had apprenticed in the studio of an established architect. It is no accident that these houses appeared at a time when architects were graduating from architecture schools at a greater rate than ever before. The Massachusetts Institute of Technology offered architecture courses as early as 1868, and Harvard began granting architecture degrees in 1895.

Almost all the houses discussed or illustrated here are clad, wholly or partially, in stucco. Not all stucco houses are English-derived Arts and Crafts in feeling or design: many of the period were in the Spanish Mission, half-timbered Tudor, Italianate, or, less frequently, Dutch Colonial styles. On the other hand, there are many Arts and Crafts houses erected in frame, brick, or stone that I have not discussed here. I chose to illustrate the style with stucco houses because they frequently demonstrated a refusal to rely on the then popular historic styles for their imagery. Their clean lines and smooth exteriors clearly reveal their architects' design ideas, and they made for a pleasingly coherent group.

Architects chose stucco because the material was the easiest and least expensive method of reproducing the masonry buildings of the English architects they were emulating. Then too, they were influenced by the stark but somehow cozy English roughcast, a more heavily textured version of our stucco. Houses built by the English architect C. F. A. Voysey often used whitewashed roughcast to clad his houses, and this surface treatment gradually gained popular acceptance in England and in the United States. The stucco finish lent to the buildings a simplicity and solidity the architects admired. They also appreciated how light played on the surface, especially if shadows of nearby plantings could soften the view.

Stucco was most often applied over frame construction, but in the early twentieth century, concrete block and structural terracotta, relatively new materials, began to be used for domestic architecture. I was accordingly surprised to find architects designing a major stucco-over-terracotta-block house in Newton, in a series of houses at a planned development for workmen in Boston, and a stucco-covered concrete block development for people of modest means built in Salem after the Great Fire of 1914.

This volume differs from previous books or articles on the Arts and Crafts of the United States in several ways. Few of them are concerned with domestic architecture influenced by English practitioners. The first to study the subject in depth was David Gebhard, who contributed a ground-breaking piece on C. F. A. Voysey's effect on American architects, although it was primarily concerned with his nineteenth century work. James C. Massey and Shirley Maxwell distinguished the English from the other American strands in a very accessible article, "English Arts and Crafts Houses in America" published in *Old-House Journal* in 2005.[4]

They discussed the "English-y" houses along the east coast in New York, Baltimore, New Jersey, and Pennsylvania, but mentioned no houses farther north than Providence. Ellen Spencer published an excellent article on Robert Voit's work in Winchester (2007); Susan Maycock and Charles Sullivan, in their *Building Old Cambridge*, write with verve and much insight about twentieth century examples of the style, but their valuable discussion is limited to the architecture of the city they explained so well.

Professor Maureen Meister, in *Architecture and the Arts and Crafts Movement in Boston* (2003) and *Arts and Crafts Architecture: History and Heritage in New England*, (2014) has written with much scholarship on the subject but touches only lightly on twentieth century houses in Massachusetts. Alan Hewitt in *The Architect and the American Country House* (1990) denied their existence, at least for country houses, saying "It is . . . not appropriate to speak of a separate Arts and Crafts mode for American country houses."[5] I eagerly awaited the 2013 edition of Virginia McAlester's wrist-bendingly comprehensive *A Field Guide to American Houses*, promoted as the "definitive guide," but she only briefly mentions the English-derived Arts and Crafts movement, states it resulted in two distinctive styles in the United States—the Prairie and Craftsman, and presents illustrations under the heading of the Tudor style for just two Arts and Crafts houses, both with false thatched roofs. Perhaps because their number is small, or they have not been seen as significant, scholars of the period have given these houses scant attention.

My approach uses original articles, photographs, and plans from early twentieth century architectural journals and wide-circulation magazines to show the reaction of the critics and architects of the period to these new houses. Because the voices of the writers are so distinctive and precise, I often quote them extensively. Research has strikingly revealed how early twentieth century Massachusetts residents felt they were embarked on a very different manner of living from that of the previous century. As these houses deserve to be seen without alterations, I have presented them in photographs of the period whenever possible.

To illustrate the sense of change, I have sought to show the forces at play in American society, including the growth of new neighborhoods in cities and in suburbs near them; the effect of new technologies and new materials on the architecture; the greater informality of the social scene that meant the near elimination of the parlor; the labor-saving devices that required fewer servants to run a household; and the growing influence of English landscape planning. Although American architects were influenced by English work, it is important to take account of their differences. While English Arts and Crafts architects were deeply interested in the well-being of workers, and several spent much time in designing affordable houses for the lower and middle classes, American architects did not generally express interest in these issues. I found only one Massachusetts Arts and Crafts style development of houses designed for laborers, although another was designed for Salem residents living on modest budgets.

A signal feature of the English Arts and Crafts movement was the focus on using local materials and hand-crafted furnishing and décor. Yet, from historic photographs and what I have observed, Massachusetts interiors show scant attention to handcrafted elements incorporated into the structure, although homeowners may have displayed any number of crafted objects and textiles in their homes. In addition, much of the interior decoration was stylistically Colonial Revival rather than more traditionally Arts and Crafts.

Another set of differences between the English models and the American adaptations reflects the differences between two countries' values and social mores. Massachusetts architects adapted their houses to our climate, and to smaller sites. Their clients did not require privacy from the road and cared less about creating artistic gardens. They did not appreciate the large living halls the English were so fond of, nor the creative solutions to the small house that featured a living room with separate alcoves for dining and reading.

However, the Massachusetts architects who drew their inspiration from such English architects as Sir Edwin Lutyens, C. F. A. Voysey, and the firm of Parker and Unwin did adapt much of their aesthetic and building vocabulary. Like their peers in California, who made Japanese and Medieval architectural building techniques their own, the Massachusetts architects who built English Arts and Crafts style houses adapted this foreign style and even underlying philosophy to American requirements. It will be the work of this book to explore how this came to be.

Why should we pay attention to these English-inspired Arts and Crafts houses? Because, at their best, they are inventive, and, using the favorite adjective of early twentieth century architects and writers about the style, "charming." Most look inviting rather than intimidating, and thus democratic instead of aristocratic, suggesting a hominess and freshness of approach that were the goals of the Massachusetts Arts and Crafts architects and their clients.

❧ **Notes** ❧

1   The Massachusetts Historical Commission erroneously allows Arts and Crafts as a subset of the Craftsman style, but it is not a searchable term under "Styles" in the Commission's master database of inventoried properties in the state.

2   Margaret Henderson Floyd, *Architecture After Richardson: Regionalism Before Modernism—Longfellow, Alden and Harlow in Boston and Pittsburgh* (Chicago: University of Chicago Press, 1994), 372.

3   James D. Kornwolf, *M. H. Baillie Scott and the Arts and Crafts Movement* (Baltimore: Johns Hopkins Press, 1972), 347.

4   James C. Massey and Shirley Maxwell, "English Arts and Crafts Houses in America," *The Old-House Journal* (February 2005), 82.

5   Mark Alan Hewitt. *The Architect and the American Country House:1890–1940* (New Haven: Yale University Press, 1990), 79.

Chapter One
THE ENGLISH AESTHETIC AND MODELS FOR AMERICAN ARCHITECTS

A curious fact about the Arts and Crafts movement in England and the United States is its strange amalgam of tradition and modernity. The architects practicing in the mode insisted that they were working with ancient vernacular forms while using the most contemporary, even forward-looking, ways of expressing them. This dualism or pairing of opposites was difficult for some to appreciate but it gave necessary meaning and freshness to their best work.

English Theory and Design Models

To understand the genesis of Arts and Crafts domestic architecture in Massachusetts it is necessary to examine the work of the theorists and architects in England, from which it sprang. Many twentieth century American critics and architects firmly believed that they could not do better than to learn from the English, although they insisted they had no wish to copy their architecture. The English architects who inspired the American designers to make their own adaptations of British models accomplished their seminal work from the 1890s through the first decade of the twentieth century, but they were, in turn, critically influenced by the much earlier art critic John Ruskin (1819–1900) and master craftsman and poet William Morris (1834–1896). So it is to these grandfathers of the Arts and Crafts movement that we must first turn.

Ruskin, a prolific author, published his two most influential books addressing building in a burst between 1849 and 1853. The strong hold that his *The Lamp of Architecture* and *The Stones of Venice* had on architects on both sides of the Atlantic may be difficult for contemporary readers to understand, much less to appreciate. His wildly elaborate, inflated rhetoric, portentous but vague generalizations, rampant religiosity and ready moralism make it difficult for us to seriously credit his ideas. But that is exactly what susceptible young aesthetes of the 1850s through the first decade of the twentieth century did.

The reason his ideas spoke so meaningfully was that he vividly and cogently identified the ugliness, mechanization, and social disruptions the Industrial Revolution in England had produced, and went on to articulate the reasons for his violently negative reaction to its gym-crack products and to the degraded conditions of its laboring classes. On a positive note, he was able to distill his aesthetic arguments in vivid, memorable language. Many who cared about architecture and handicraft came to agree with his analysis and precepts.

Perhaps his major principle concerned truth in building. "In architecture another . . . more contemptible, violation of truth is possible: a direct falsity of assertion respecting the nature of material, or the quantity of labour."[1] The deceits

FIGURE 1.1 Red House, Bexleyheath, London (Philip Webb, 1859). Webb's seminal Arts and Crafts house for William Morris was more Gothic than its followers.

he meant were a suggested structural support rather than the real one, painting a surface to represent another surface, as in marbling, and "The use of cast or machine-made ornaments of any kind."[2] It was not, he thought, the material "but the absence of human labour, which makes the thing worthless."[3] This also applied to stucco, although we will find that stucco was a signature feature of the English-inspired Arts and Crafts domestic architecture in Massachusetts.

Another was his insistence that beauty sprang from an appreciation of God's work, or Nature, as the source of all structure and ornament. He typically stated, ". . . forms which are not taken from natural objects must be ugly."[4] A third was the novel idea that only independent, creative workmen, united in a common and spiritual purpose, and therefore happy workmen, could produce good work. Ruskin's insistence on honesty, organic structure as well as ornament, and handcrafted work became the basic tenet of the Arts and Crafts movement, though his virtual prohibition of machine-manufactured elements became more honored in the breach than in fact.

A significant target of his reprobation was the English classical building tradition that included its beloved Georgian period. He saw this major swath of architectural styles as based on the infidel Greek and Roman cultures: only the Gothic, and not all of that, was appropriate for a Christian nation such as England. Last, one of the first preservationists, he advocated the care and protection of English historic buildings, mainly its Gothic and early vernacular houses. However, he was violently in favor of conservation and as strongly against the restoration of any ancient building on the grounds that its value lay in a building's apparent age: restoration would introduce new materials and so destroy its expressiveness.

If John Ruskin's influence was theoretical, the prodigiously talented William Morris provided practical grounding for the movement on many fronts: through his writings; the house he built for his family; his leadership of the Art Workers Guild (1889), Arts and Crafts Exhibition Society (1888), and the impressive number and quality of still-famous handcrafted products his firms produced between 1861 and his death in 1896. Ironically, so popular have been his designs for the past decade that they are now mass-produced as paper plates, tea towels, umbrellas, wallets, business cards, and iPhone cases.

The Red House Morris commissioned for his family from architect Philip Webb in 1859 (see Figure 1.1) became the first Arts and Crafts house and a seminal building in the movement's world. Webb and Morris turned the recommendations from Ruskin's 1854 Edinburgh Lectures into beautiful red brick.[5] It was all there, the medieval imperative, liberally sprinkled with the Gothic arches the author recommended over conventional rectangular windows and the steep gable roofs, one that even descended asymmetrically down two floors, which would become a signature gesture in the domestic architecture that followed. But the design was so simplified and abstracted as to be almost a-historic, a revolutionary turn in a period of ornate Italianate villas or heavily garnished Neo-Gothic houses. Morris and his Pre-Raphaelite friends painted the interior walls, ceilings, and furniture with romantic medievalist murals, the first step in his career of showing the way to use crafts as the most important element in home furnishing.

Born to a wealthy family and an Oxford graduate, Morris became convinced that understanding a craft required one to practice it. So he taught himself textile and wallpaper design and manufacture, typography, printing, bookbinding embroidery, tapestry, and stained-glass making. As the head of a succession of firms first established in 1861, he manufactured wallpaper and textiles, making beautifully designed products accessible to middle- and upper-class homeowners who would otherwise have had to purchase the remarkably overwrought home furnishings that were spewed out by the industrial system we now label "Victorian." His papers and textiles were Medieval in feeling, ornate enough to meet the taste of Victorian buyers but, although highly artistic and hand produced, were nevertheless manufactured products that could be made with variety and in quantities. His democratizing socialist ideas and promotion of the notion that beauty could lie in the simplicity of well-made handmade objects affected Arts and Crafts architects indirectly but powerfully.

Morris, a polymath, eventually became involved in the re-creation of the medieval guild system of production. In spite of his efforts and other prominent Arts and Crafts architects of a similar bent, the late nineteenth and early twentieth century English guilds, meant to restore independence and respect to craftspeople, were unable to compete against industrialized manufactured products. One of Morris's achievements was that he found a way to make products within the economic reach of the upper middle class, in contrast to the time-consuming crafts made by guild members affordable only by the very rich. Morris, the activist, took up Ruskin's stricture to preserve the nation's historic architecture, in part protest against inept "restorations" by insensitive architects. He characteristically acted on the idea, cofounding with Pre-Raphaelite friends in 1877 the still active Society for the Preservation of Ancient Buildings.

Strangely, Ruskin's and Morris's ideas did not perceptibly affect the British architects practicing in the 1860s through the 1880s, who generally practiced in a decorative Queen Anne style. Skipping a generation, it fell to the young architects of the 1890s and the first decade of the new century to take up their artistic strictures as a radical return to simplicity, honesty, and Englishness. These were the men who joined or were close to the English Arts and Crafts Exhibition of 1888 or the Art Workers Guild founded the same year. The most respected of them were Edwin Lutyens, C. F. A. Voysey, the firm of Parker and Unwin, and, less influential in America, M. H. Baillie Scott.

It was the designs of these men and their peers that, after a lag in crossing the Atlantic, inspired many American architects to base their work on several characteristics of the English movement. They saw its pared-down simplicity as modern and appropriate for the new mores and technology of forward-looking America of the twentieth century. In particular, Massachusetts architects were attracted to the sturdy shapes of English vernacular buildings and chose to use these models instead of the current fixation on "correct" historic styles. However, while in theory they wanted to emulate the English architects' strikingly honest use of building materials and their organic integration of architecture and craftsmanship, the Americans were not always able to incorporate these ideals.

⊰ The International Context for the Arts and Crafts Movement ⊱

The revolution that was the English Arts and Crafts movement occurred in the context of the cultural upheavals taking place in many Western countries. The years between the turn of the twentieth century and the start of World War I in 1914 were heady ones for European arts. Avant-garde artists were producing revolutionary works: in dance, Diaghilev, Fokine, and Duncan; in music Stravinsky, Debussy, and Ravel; in the visual arts, Picasso, Rousseau, Klimt, and Mondrian; in literature, Proust, Yeats, Pound, and D. H. Lawrence; and in architecture, Gaudi, Hoffmann, and Wagner. All were shaking up the known forms and making work experienced as violently new and often disturbing.

⊰ The English Models ⊱

Charles Francis Annesley Voysey, usually referred to as C. F. A. Voysey, (1857–1941) was highly influential for English as well as American architects and their clients. According to Hermann Muthesius, a singularly observant and insightful German diplomat and architect who described early twentieth century English architecture while it was being created, Voysey was the best known of his group of iconoclasts. His houses were deeply personal or individualistic and startlingly modern to turn-of-the-twentieth century eyes.

Like his contemporary Frank Lloyd Wright, born ten years later, Voysey believed the architect must take responsibility for all aspects of house design, including interior finishes, furni-

FIGURE 1.2 Perrycroft, Colwall, Worcestershire (C. F. A. Voysey, 1894). This charming house was a model for the long, hip-roofed, horizontally massed houses in Massachusetts, whose architects sometimes copied its overhanging second story and full buttresses.

ture, and decoration. And like Wright, he took to new heights the idea of simplicity in design. In discussing the meaning of simplicity, which he prized above all, Voysey brought up his dearly held values, "In most modern drawing rooms confusion is the first thing that strikes one. Nowhere is there breath, dignity, repose or true richness of effect, but a symbolism of money alone."[6] And like Wright, Voysey again and again stressed the necessity of the horizontal

FIGURE 1.3 The Orchard, Chorley Wood, Hertfordshire (C. F. A. Voysey, 1899). The motif of two high-pitched gables flanking a hip roof was attractive to Massachusetts architects who employed it frequently to give interest to a façade. They copied Voysey's catslide roof at the right of the photograph, but not the eight-foot ceilings he made low to provide coziness and reflect light back into the rooms. See also Figure 4.7 Pine Road, Brookline, and Figure 4.2 1547 Centre Street, Newton.

FIGURE 1.4 The White Cottage, 68 Lyford Road, London (C. F. A. Voysey, 1903). Because it sits on a modest London lot, this is one of Voysey's more restrained designs.

line, which he identified with the all-important quality of repose.

Muthesius, however, was incorrect in his belief that Voysey's designs totally abandoned historical tradition; in fact, his houses were partly based on the English vernacular cottages the architect seemed to revere. But he was right in identifying the principal characteristics of Voysey's houses: long, low proportions; the use of roughcast plaster, a form of heavily pebbled stucco walls; roofs that project far beyond the wall resting on slender wrought-iron brackets and "strips of small, narrow windows."[7] (See Figure 1.2.) His tapering buttresses became almost a trademark, although

other architects used them as well. Voysey employed buttresses not to mimic Medieval architecture but to actually brace the stucco-covered nine-inch brick walls, and also to add shadows to the elevations and break up the massing.

To this list can be added several other characteristics—arched entries, and the eye-catching gable roof beginning at its high peak and sweeping down to ground-floor-window height, what I shall term a cat-slide roof. (See Figure 1.3.) These features were reused by Massachusetts architects, though few sustained Voysey's austerity. It is easy to understand why local architects rejected Voysey's improbably low, seven-and-one-half or eight-foot high ceilings, planned for coziness and to reflect light into the room.

What seemed to appeal to most American architects in Voysey's works were his ascetic but somehow cozy forms,

FIGURE 1.5 Munstead Wood, Godalming, Surrey (Edwin Lutyens, 1896–1897). Note the massive exterior chimneys, prominent catslide roof, banded windows, and discreet use of half-timbering. One image cannot convey the complexity of this design, different from every point of view.

THE ENGLISH AESTHETIC AND MODELS FOR AMERICAN ARCHITECTS

the white-stuccoed surfaces of which simplified the massing, and, together with masterful window placement, figured heavily in emphasizing the satisfying proportions of his houses. Voysey's White Cottage of 1903 at 68 Lyford Road, London (see Figure 1.4), illustrates one of his less known, and most traditional examples. The plainness of his design was achieved against a tradition of a great deal of ornamentation. It must have taken much bravery to nearly eliminate exterior ornament and let the honest construction speak for itself.

Voysey's skill in integrating plan and façade would be difficult to replicate, but that did not stop American architects from trying, often at a reduced scale. American Arts and Crafts architects, however, never attempted to reproduce his expensive stone mullions (uprights dividing window panes) and window and door surrounds that give Voysey's houses their coexisting air of medieval antiquity and stark modernity. Instead they focused, when clients allowed, on introducing casement windows with leaded glass panes.

Edwin Landseer Lutyens, (1869–1944) one of Britain's leading architects, began his career in close cooperation with his first important client, the pioneering and eventually renowned landscape designer Gertrude Jekyll (1843–1932). She taught him to envision the house and garden as one unit, each enhancing the other. Munstead Wood was to be Jekyll's own home, she wanted a house that would offer her a gracious and comfortable experience rather than serve as a showplace to impress others. In his early work, the architect succeeded in achieving a remarkably homey atmosphere and equally impressive, but quite different, front and garden elevations, using simplified, nearly unornamented vernacular forms. Beautifully made stone walls contrasted with small areas of half-timbering, bold gabled dormers with cat-slide roofs, and boldly recessed porches enlivened the massing. Small-paned banked or ribbons of casement windows and massive exterior chimneys were characteristics that would reappear, in altered form, in a majority of the Arts and Crafts house of Massachusetts some years later (see Figure 1.5).

Ms. Jekyll wrote glowingly of Lutyen's 1897 Munstead Wood's naturalness, honesty, simplicity, repose, and tradition, all standard Arts and Crafts movement values. She thought, "it had taken to itself the soul of a more ancient dwelling place. The house is not in any way a copy of any old building though it embodies the general characteristics of the older structures of its own district."[8] The cultural critic Elizabeth Outka[9] points out that the owners of Lutyens' new-old country houses were purchasing, and the readers of the magazines in which they were published were attracted to, a particular form of nostalgia for an authentically "English," preindustrial past with links to the nobility who might have inhabited them, had they really been ancient. It is no wonder that the architect received numerous commissions for large country estates from rich businessmen, or that he gave up the Arts and Crafts mode and turned to conservative classical and Georgian Revivalist styles later in his career.

His much bigger house of the following year, Orchards, made use of asymmetrical massing, a high hip roof, a buttressed wall, a two-story bay window, and high-placed windows. American architects, when they emulated these attractive, dramatic features, tended to reduce them in size for a scale appropriate for the middle-class house rather than for the manor house for an authentic English country gentleman.

If Lutyens specialized in large country houses for upper class clients and Voysey in smaller and often summer houses for a more modest group, partners Barry Parker and Raymond Unwin specialized in creating housing for workers in Garden Cities and suburbs. The architects, second cousins, brothers-in-law, and ardent socialists, were committed to keeping housing costs at a minimum so that workers could afford an attractive house.

The Garden City concept was the brainchild of Ebenezer

FIGURE 1.6 Parker and Unwin Office, 296 Norton Way South, Letchworth Garden City (Parker and Unwin, 1907). Parker & Unwin's office had a real thatched roof, unlike most other buildings in the suburb they designed. But it was intended to set the tone for combining the new, architect-designed buildings with ancient and vernacular practice, and to model several design motifs. In this it succeeded brilliantly.

Howard, a utopian and social reformer whose first book in 1898, republished in 1902 as *Garden Cities of To-Morrow*, set out how a city or town, removed by a greenbelt from the central city, could accommodate laborers and displaced farm workers in healthy, beautiful, and completely planned environments. Parker and Unwin were hired in 1902 to make Howard's vision a reality, essentially to plan and design Letchworth Garden City. Because the founders envisioned for the new city a wide range of classes, while many of the houses were designed to be affordable enough for working class families, others were scaled for the upper middle class. Ironically, many of the houses were too expensive for the workers and middle-classes for which they were designed: the town soon attracted the more well to do and today, the pleasant, leafy place is the choice of celebrities.

Howard's radical social ideas did not immediately translate to developments in the United States, but Letchworth's housing stock, designed by many independent architects as well as Parker and Unwin, became a storehouse of Arts and Crafts motifs for American architects. One such motif was the picturesque thatched roof, so iconic of English vernacular cottages. Although they yearned to possess the cachet of authentic "Englishness" and the charm of ancient buildings, the Americans lacked not only the thatching and capable roofers, they were unable to use the flammable material due to zoning laws. Instead, American architects were forced to reinterpret this organic material with manufactured asphalt shingle or slate, imitating the curved line of thatching in "rolled roofs" or its undulating movement over dormer windows with what I term "false thatch" eaves treatments (see Figure 1.6).

Unwin, who began as an engineer, took over the town planning aspects of the scheme, introducing innovative streetscapes and grouped siting plans that were widely copied. (One such development located on the outskirts of Boston for local workmen's families, is discussed in Chapter 5.)

Several of Letchworth Garden City's design motifs such as bay and bow windows, small-paned windows, and multiple gables, were holdovers from the preceding Queen Anne style. Others included Voysey's much-copied gestures such as his plain roughcast walls (a more textured version of our stucco), steeply pitched and cat-slide roofs, marked horizontality, and bands of casement windows. But due to the use of old, ingrained vernacular forms combined with the bold simplicity of shapes and absence of superficial applied decoration, the Arts and Crafts designs looked both reassuringly familiar and modern enough for the twentieth century (see Figure 1.7).

Beside stressing the importance of good materials, fine workmanship, and honest structure, the overarching value these Arts and Crafts architects tried to achieve in their designs was the quality of unstudied vernacular architecture and ad hoc village planning found in ancient villages. They were committed to producing modern work that could be seen as "charming," "quaint, "picturesque," and "homey." These words became ubiquitous, even hackneyed, in descriptions of both English building and their English-inspired American houses. The utterly practical Raymond Unwin, in commenting on the organic order found in ancient English settlements, stated the obvious when he said

"Certainly where many buildings and sizes are gathered together, as in a village, a picturesqueness of grouping is rarely absent even when the individual buildings have in themselves no special beauty . . ."[10]

Parker and Unwin also designed Arts and Crafts houses that tended to be more formal and unburdened by features difficult to reproduce. An example is their house in another planned development (see Figure 1.8). The only slightly asymmetrical door placement in an arched, recessed entry were appealing features for American architects to offer homeowners more used to symmetrical Colonial house forms. And Massachusetts clients slowly came to accept the casement windows and striking wall dormers, although without their distinctive hip roofs.

I have focused on a few of the most prominent and imitated Arts and Crafts practitioners,

FIGURE 1.7 1 & 2 Eastholm, Wilbury Road, Letchworth Garden City (Parker & Unwin, 1905–1906). One of a simple but gracefully designed pair of semidetached houses in Letchworth Garden City; the other is tucked away around the corner. The gesture locating the arched front door under the catslide roof of the gabled entry was frequently replicated in Letchworth Garden City and in Massachusetts.

FIGURE 1.8 25 Asmuns Hill Road, Hampstead Garden Suburb, Hertfordshire (Parker & Unwin, 1909). This house with its subtle details and near absence of historical motifs could almost be at home in a Massachusetts suburb. Local architects adopted its distinctive through-the-eaves dormers and high hip roof, though without the thick roof tile. In general, Hampstead's architecture tended to the formality of the Georgian Revival, which might explain the appeal of this house for American architects.

but the British Isles held dozens of creative architects who helped round out the style. They include such men as C. R. Ashbee, W. R. Lethaby, M. H. Baillie Scott, Detmar Blow, William H. Bidlake, C. R. Mackintosh, Earnest Newton, and E. S. Prior. Less well-known architects such as Walter Brierly, Mervyn Macartney, Walter Cave, and others too numerous to mention, helped build a body of work that is still admirable and still studied.

In England, the Arts and Crafts movement was essentially finished by the inception of World War I. Building was at a standstill and the popular taste had moved on to the Georgian Revival that had never really been abandoned. Ironically, speaking of the decline of the movement, and of Parker and Unwin's work, one scholar commented, "Abandoned by architects, the forms were adopted by speculative builders and local authorities. Round every sizable town in England there is a ring of Arts and Crafts suburbs where, following planning rules drawn up by Unwin, . . . the architecture of Voysey, Baillie Scott, Parker and early Lutyens lives on in endless copies of hips and gables, half-timbering . . ., mullions and leaded bay windows. . . . The builders did what the architects, for all their high ideals, failed to accomplish. They brought Arts & Crafts to the people."[11]

These were only a few of the many movement architects practicing in England, but their work was probably the most inspiring to Arts and Crafts designers in Massachusetts. Their seminal designs were the most striking and the most easily adaptable of all the built forms the architects of the Commonwealth encountered in the extensive architectural literature of the time or visited in person.

1 John Ruskin, *The Lamp of Beauty: Writings on Art*, ed. Joan Evans (London: Phaidon Press, 1995), 201.

2 Ibid., 202.

3 Ibid., 202.

4 Ibid., 214.

5 Jaques Migeon, "The Red House and Ruskin," http://www.morrissociety.org/publications/JWMS/SP77.3.3.Migeon.pdf. I am indebted to Jaques Migeon for this insight into the relationship of the Red House to Ruskin's Edinburgh Lectures.

6 Voysey, C. F. A., "Interview with Mr. Charles Francis Annesley Voysey," *The Studio* (London, 1893), 234.

7 Hermann Muthesius, *The English House*, ed. Dennis Sharp (New York: Rizzoli, 1987), 42.

8 Gertrude Jekyll, *Home and Garden*. Quoted in O'Neill, Daniel, *Lutyens: Country Houses* (London: Lund Humphries, 1980), 31–32.

9 Elizabeth Outka, *Consuming Traditions: Modernity, Modernism, and the Commodified Authentic* (New York: Oxford University Press), 2009.

10 Raymond Unwin, "Of Co-Operation in Building," in Barry Parker and Raymond Unwin, *The Art of Building a Home: A Collection of Lectures and Illustrations* (London: Longmans, Green and Co., 1901), 92.
    https://archive.org/stream/artofbuildinghomoopark/artofbuildinghomoopark_djvu.txt

11 Peter Davey, *Arts and Crafts Architecture: The Search for Earthly Paradise* (London: The Architectural Press, 1980), 191.

Chapter Two
THE ENGLISH INFLUENCE AND AMERICAN ADAPTATIONS

Architecture may be the most responsive of all the arts to changes in the social fabric of the community and the aesthetic sensibilities of its residents. And domestic architecture, although essentially conservative, must in some sense mirror the society that pays for it. What forces were at work that made English-inspired Arts and Crafts houses popular during the first two decades of twentieth century Massachusetts?

⌐ Setting the Stage for Arts and Crafts Houses in Massachusetts ⌐

Certainly, the residents of eastern Massachusetts were both historically and aspirationally Anglophiles as in no other area of the country. Many impulses supported this identification: first, England had principally populated the Colony and Commonwealth, ruled its inhabitants for over one-hundred and fifty years, and, in spite of the colony's rebellion, served as the source of good taste thereafter. Second, in the early twentieth century, it was a generally acknowledged belief that the British were the world's best masters of homebuilding. Last, by identifying with the English and adopting their styles, the middle and upper classes sought to distinguish themselves from the poorer, less-educated Irish, Italian, eastern European, and Jewish immigrants that had been pouring into Boston since the mid-nineteenth century.

In fact, the first owner of a 1908 Arts and Crafts house in Brookline, Prescott Farnsworth Hall, was a leader in the battle to keep non-Anglo Saxon "ignorant foreigners" from polluting or diluting the native population. It is not surprising that he would choose a rather formal English Arts and Crafts house to express his intense anglophile identification. A founding member of the Boston-based Immigration Restriction League in 1894, and a Brahmin Harvard-trained lawyer, Hall successfully urged the passage of the nativist Federal Immigration Act of 1917. An eight-dollar tax on each immigrant and a literacy test did much to exclude immigrants from Asia, southern and eastern Europe, and Jews.[1]

Architects were among the most prominent in proclaiming the superiority of English homes. Warren Langford, the first dean of Harvard's School of Architecture and an early supporter of the English Arts and Crafts movement, gushed,

"It is not too much to say that no other nation has succeeded in developing a domestic architecture having the subtle and intimate charm which in the English country house makes so strong an appeal to the love of home as well as to the love of beauty. Its serene dignity, its air of protecting seclusion, its cozy home-likeness, its quiet and restrained beauty, its close sympathy with the surrounding landscape, its simplicity, are the very expression of all that is best in English domestic life."[2]

Born in England himself, Langford's tacit assumption was that English domestic life, as well as the architecture that expressed it, was superior to those of all other nations.

Massachusetts architect Allen W. Jackson, who often used English half-timbering in his sensitively designed twentieth century Massachusetts houses, inserted a racial note: "England is the pre-eminent land for country houses and their subtle instinct for hearth and home is our rightful heritage, and strikes a racial chord so deep as to elude analysis."[3] Another Massachusetts architect, J. Lovell Little Jr. argued that the English combined a larger amount than our average house of the "domestic qualities suggesting a home" and the "harmonizing of the needs of the client with the natural setting of the house . . . that brings peace and comfort to the occupants . . . and gives an outsider the pleasure that one has in any well-balanced view of a picture."[4]

For their country houses however, the very richest Massachusetts residents preferred to take their cue from European palaces of the nobility. MIT graduate and Brookline resident, architect Robert Day Andrews, in 1904, attributed this proclivity to "the sudden creation of a distinct wealthy class." He saw "the new plutocratic type of country house"[5] as an embrace of autocracy and formalism rather than the English love of freedom, domesticity, and informal plan. But the socially prominent and unfortunately racist Boston architect was not afraid that "the mass of our people would forget the English ideal" because "[t]he amount of Latin blood in the American people is very small compared to the Teutonic or northern European races, and heredity and influences are more powerful and lasting than environment."[6]

Authors in the early years of the twentieth century stressed that Massachusetts was more English than other area of the country. Speaking of Boston, one architect stated, "in no other city have both client and architect a more decided *penchant* for the style of their English ancestors. The result is that the suburbs of Boston, Brookline, Beverly, Wenham etc. all suggest without actually repeating, rural England."[7] A forthrightly bigoted critic insisted that "Boston remains the most English of American cities—the most English and at the same time the most Irish. The alien influences enter in the shape of Italians and Jews, but their effect is not overwhelming as it is in New York."[8]

One sign-posted indication of suburban Boston's English identification is the disproportionate number of English or Scottish-derived street names they contain. For example, Brookline and Newton, neighboring suburbs with the highest number of English Arts and Crafts houses, both contain non-contiguous public ways named Cotswold, Devon, and Grasmere. In addition, Brookline included Allandale, Buckminster, Glencoe, Heath, Monmouth, Somerset, Strathmore, Verndale, Waverly, and York; while Newton could offer Anglophiles a house on Albermarle, Albion, Arundel, Blithdale, Croftdale, Fellsmere, Gladstonbury, Hampshire, Hereford, Highland Park, Islington, and Ivanhoe, to suggest only a small sample.

A unique combination of forces in the early twentieth century made conditions ripe for the success of the English style: the wide availability of images; descriptions and commentary on contemporary English Arts and Crafts houses; a larger and better-informed group of local architects knowledgeable about English styles, and the rapid growth of the suburbs with their attractive, relatively inexpensive land, larger lots, and rapid access to the city.

⁂ Challenges for Arts and Crafts Houses ⁂

The would-be homeowners of Massachusetts and their architects were faced with a number of problems to overcome in replicating English Arts and Crafts houses. Although so close in many respects, in the almost two-and-one-half centuries since English immigrants had put an ocean between themselves and their homeland, and the one-and-a-quarter in which Massachusetts had become part of a new, melting-pot nation, the experience of the two countries had diverged markedly.

Perhaps it was the opening of the twentieth century that seemed to require a shift from the past: new ways of life, new technologies, and new ideas that called for a refreshing new form of home building. The eight issues listed below mark both the challenges and achievements of the English Arts and Crafts style in Massachusetts.

1. English Arts and Crafts architects generally relied on Medieval and Gothic architecture for their models. However, New England had very few medieval houses and only faint Gothic examples such as the high-peaked gable roofs of Salem's House of Seven Gables. The handful that had survived into the twentieth century was generally small, modest, and not often disposed in picturesque groupings. Thus, Americans had to borrow from abroad for their vernacular models.

2. The early American houses were erected in cheap, abundant wood rather than the preponderantly masonry materials of the ancient English examples. Moreover, the English based their designs on a catalogue of vernacular architectures that had each grown from a particular heritage, geography, and location, with unique building techniques, materials, and house forms. In contrast, Massachusetts had a limited vernacular tradition with little variety, though the tradition and materials did differ in Pennsylvania and the New York/New Jersey area.

3. The plans evolved by English Arts & Crafts architects were often unsuitable for more informal American mores and tastes.

4. Except for a few very large English country houses, the smaller houses, often called "cottages," were usually too simple and unassuming for very wealthy Americans to emulate, the patrons best able to employ architects familiar with English Arts and Crafts architecture. Very rich owners might use the Arts and Crafts style to house

their chauffer and gardener, but would choose the more pretentious Georgian Revival, French Renaissance, or Spanish Mission for their own mansions.

5. The early Arts & Crafts English theorists despised the machine for the social disenfranchisement of its workers and equally for the displacement of handmade articles and the individuality of handmade building. Americans were in love with machinery: no architect practicing in New England could dispense with machine-made materials and industrial techniques. And, while an Arts and Crafts aesthetic did develop in New England, craftwork was primarily the product of upper-class women who wove, made pottery, book bindings, and small metal objects that were crafted to furnish the house rather than become integrated into its structure.

6. Beginning with the United States Centennial of 1876, and after their romance with the fanciful and ornate Queen Anne style had lost much of its popularity, Americans wholeheartedly adopted the more sedate Colonial Georgian and Federal styles as patriotic and national symbols, especially in New England. Thus, the American image of home was essentially a formal, often highly decorated, classically inspired envelope, not an asymmetrical, low-slung masonry building punctuated by bow, casement, or strips of windows.

7. Americans of the early twentieth century had an impressive number of styles to choose from for their new houses. A book on country houses published in 1912, discussed "the Modern English Plaster House"—our English Arts and Crafts, as just one of nine other options: Colonial, Swiss Chalet, Italian Adaptations, Tudor, Spanish Mission, Half-Timber, Dutch Colonial, "Style of the Western Plains," and houses of the "Northern Tradition." Truly, the Arts and Crafts style had an unprecedented number of styles with which to compete.

8. None of the Arts & Crafts architects practicing in New England, with the possible exceptions of Frank Chouteau Brown, J. Lovell Little Jr., and Allen Jackson, were theorists or even spokesmen for the movement. And because Arts and Crafts domestic architecture in England was never a style but an attitude towards building and a series of gestures and proportions, the lack of an identifiable group did not make for a readily distinctive brand. Perhaps this made the spread of Arts and Crafts architecture more limited. A second result of the disinclination of Massachusetts architects to write about their design ideas is that they left a relatively scanty record of the architectural influences that shaped the buildings they designed.

All these difficulties made the architect-designed examples of the English-inspired Arts and Crafts house few in number but necessarily distinctively American. Their influence, however, spread in the 1920s and 1930s so that ordinary builders' models, using stucco for typical foursquare plans and high-peaked, catslide-roofed entry pavilions became common features in expanding city neighborhoods and burgeoning suburbs across Massachusetts.

⁙ Conditions Contributing to the Spread of English-Inspired Arts and Crafts Houses ⁙

How did a relatively new movement, not even a well-articulated style and from a foreign country, make headway in tradition-inclined Massachusetts? Certainly, the increase in well-trained local architects exposed to recent developments here and abroad became a factor in the popularity of the English Arts and Crafts style. Writing in 1907, a critic claimed that, more than any city but one, Boston had "a greater number of men capable of producing domestic work of such originality . . . that is generally easy to distinguish their houses at a glance from the ruck and commonplace."[9]

Architecture schools associated with Boston universities became a major source of training for these fledgling architects. The Massachusetts Institute of Technology offered architectural courses in 1868, the first in the United States to do so. Its long history of rigorous, professional education helped it to become a leading educator of architects in Boston. A majority of houses discussed in this book are by architects who attended MIT.

Harvard, in 1874, first included the immensely popular fine arts and architectural lectures by cultural star Charles Eliot Norton. A committed Arts and Crafts enthusiast, he was close friends with and advocates for both Ruskin and Morris. It was not until 1895, however, that Harvard students could count on a series of classes oriented to professional training. Three years later the university offered an architectural degree, but only in 1913 was a distinct faculty of architecture organized.

H. Langford Warren, a founding member of the Boston Society of Arts and Crafts and its president from 1907 to 1917, was the man appointed to create Harvard's architectural program, first for the college and later for the university. Born in England and trained as an architect at MIT, he was devoted to advancing the collaboration between architects and craftsmen. However, he was not conspicuously committed to English Arts and Crafts exteriors. While he designed several houses in Cambridge, only his own house and one other possess more than a faint reference to the style.

In the wartime academic year 1914–1915, Warren's acquaintance, the distinguished Arts and Crafts English architect C. R. Ashbee, delivered the first of a lecture series at Harvard's School of Architecture on "The History and Present Practices of Country House Architecture."[10] It almost certainly concerned the English experience and very probably a generous portion of Boston's practicing architects were either in attendance or wished to be. Ashbee's lecture was followed by Allen Jackson's, whose own house on Brattle Street in Cambridge is a still intriguing example of the Massachusetts version of the style (see Figure 4.5).

Many other young men who built in the Arts and Crafts style chose the traditional route of training in the offices of leading Boston architects.[11] It would seem that after basic apprenticeship, these men were elevated to the position of head draftsman in the office of their master, and, with this on their resume, went off to form firms of their own, often with another architect trained in the same office. To put the finishing touch on their education, an even larger number than those who attended MIT chose either pre- or post-graduate study at the most prestigious institution of all, the École de Beaux Arts in Paris and its associated studios. In spite of the fact that the École taught a rigid system of classicism with formal axis, emphasis on symmetry and French sensibilities, many of these students managed to find a reason to offer their clients house designs in Arts and Crafts style upon their return to Massachusetts.

Of the approximately 141 houses built between 1903 and 1922 chosen as examples of the local Arts and Crafts style for this book,[12] I have been able to identify forty-four different architectural firms, many with several such houses to their credit.[13] This reflects not only the large number of architects practicing in the suburbs around Boston, Worcester, and Springfield, and areas popular for summer houses, but their willingness to select the English-inspired Arts and Crafts style from among all the competing styles.

These architects could count on a battery of local organizations and publications to support them in their professional life and continuing education. The august Boston Society of Architects, founded in 1867, mounted an exhibition of Voysey's work in 1891. The Boston Architectural Club gathered in 1889, and at least eight leading Boston architects served on the advisory board of the Boston Society of Arts and Crafts, founded in 1897. An exhibit, mounted in 1916, was the joint effort of the Society and the professional journal *The American Architect*. The journal's review declared that the exhibit's lay visitors were becoming better educated about architecture and that: "this unconscious education is the result of recurring exhibitions and the exploitation in illustrated magazines, of good examples of architecture would seem obvious."[14]

Professional journals played a significant role in promoting the English Arts and Crafts style, allowing architects to inform themselves via sketches, photographs, and plans of modern institutional, commercial, and domestic work, and new building techniques. Importantly, the American journals did not scant the indigenous scene, often featuring houses by local architects. This is one reason why several professional journals appeared in different areas of the country.[15] Boston became the publishing home of no less than three professional journals. *The Architectural Record* (1891), though it soon moved to New York; *The Brickbuilder* (1892) and *The Architectural Review* (1896) for which the opinionated and outspoken Arts and Crafts local architect Frank Chouteau Brown served as the longtime editor. In addition, two new influential, popular magazines were interested in English Arts and Crafts houses. *The House Beautiful* published in Chicago in 1896, published an illustrated article about a Voysey house in 1899 and another on the Garden Cities of England in 1912, among scores of similar pieces. Boston magazine *Indoors and Out* (1905–1907) ran several admiring articles on Arts and Crafts houses before being absorbed by *The House Beautiful*.

The Architectural Review, beginning in 1900, kept a steady focus on both English Arts and Crafts work in England and its appearance in Massachusetts. Like other professional publications, the *Review* routinely presented a brief summary of significant architecture covered in other journals, making the journal the primary professional advocate of the style. Not only did the *Review* publish the most articles on Arts and Crafts, it may have been the most enthusiastic about them. For example, a brief notice in 1906 opined first that architect Allen Jackson's own house in Cambridge was "particularly successful and fascinating" and in the same paragraph that Lutyen's Little Thackum house in West Sussex, England, was "so charming in every possible aspect that the reviewer declines to express himself fully on the subject."[16] The acerbic tone generally used by the *Review* can be heard in a comment in "Current Periodicals" of February 1903, "There is nothing in the *Builder's Journal* and *Architectural Record* of the month that demands particular notice, except perhaps Mr. Voysey's country house in Surry, one view of which we reprint. This is a design with all Mr. Voysey's personality and with more than the usual allowance of picturesqueness."[17]

The Brickbuilder, founded in Boston in 1892, a trade magazine for architects and builders working in brick and clay products, published two lengthy articles on "Modern British Suburban Houses" in 1906 and 1907 that featured work of prominent English Arts and Crafts architects as well as four long articles, in 1906, by Frank Chouteau Brown on "The Relationship Between English and American Domestic Architecture."

For the homeowner, home-buyer, or home-dreamer, the popular magazines were both entertaining and informative. Between 1899 and 1911, *The House Beautiful* supplied seven articles on English or English-inspired Arts and Crafts houses, the largest number by a popular magazine. Included were two prominent English architects, C. R. Ashbee in 1910 and M. H. Baillie Scott, the following year. *The Craftsman*, Gustav Stickley's magazine marketing his Craftsman houses and the simple lifestyle it promoted, published an essay in 1909 from "The Art of Building and Home" by Barry Parker and Raymond Unwin, the architects of Letchworth Garden City and Hampstead Garden Suburb. Both their aesthetic and their idea about the importance of the practical, convenient, and workable home design essentially coincided with Stickley's. Like Baillie Scott, Parker and Unwin insisted that, instead of cramming a parlor, living room, dining room into a small house, it was better to reduce the number of those rooms and combine them into one large, multiuse space. *The Craftsman* also published an illustrated article by Voysey on his own work in 1912.

In reviewing the role of publications in the spread of English-inspired Arts and Crafts houses in Massachusetts, I find it telling that almost a quarter of the houses included in this book were documented in a professional journal, popular magazine, or book, and in one case, shown in the Boston Architectural Club Exhibit of 1907. The number is extraordinary, especially as not all of the houses themselves are extraordinary. This high percentage seems to represent a real receptivity to the style by both publishers and the public.

There was no shortage of books advising readers on the design of English Arts and Crafts houses. Those published in England were apparently aimed at prospective homeowners wanting "Country Cottages and Weekend Houses"[18] or "Small Country Cottages of Today."[19] Eight such books were published in the United States, several suggesting a multitude of different styles: Aymar Embury's guide portrayed the "Modern English"; Massachusetts architect J. Lovell Little Jr. argued passionately for choosing the "Modern English Plaster House" over the seven other likely styles.[20] Little's emphasis on plaster or stucco is the first such designation.

Architect Elkin Wallick, who characterized America's Victorian architecture as "a period of abortions, both in building and decoration of houses,"[21] believed this new abundance of contemporary, illustrated literature and the public's easy access to it was responsible for the recent improvement in domestic architecture. Due to our "numerous magazines and books devoted to house building and decorating, we no longer need to remain in ignorance of such matters, for the best examples of houses, not only of this country, but of other countries, are all pictured and described and brought to our very doorsteps for our inspection."[22] The phrase "very doorsteps" says it all.

❧ Defining an English Style to Emulate ❧

American interest in learning about the English Arts and Crafts work can be judged by looking at the number of essays published in American journals and magazines by the English architects who made the work and critics who observed it. Common to these articles was a longing for a new architecture to go with a new century. In 1901, Charles Holme, founder of the English journal, *The Studio*, wrote that the last century's attempts to revive past styles principally failed because they "misrepresented modern conditions and modern requirements. The new century should generate a style characteristic of its own, borrowing from the past only those features that are in accordance with present day needs."[23]

Essays by architects Edward Prior and Parker and Unwin, among the leaders of the English movement, appeared in American publications in 1909. Instead of arguing for a new style, Prior expressed a revolutionary desire for no style. He proposed that architects "must be classed, not by the Style they copy, but by the kind of efforts they make to escape from all Styles."[24] Another class of architects recognized "that not classical allusion, but an atmosphere of Quaker-like sobriety is the condition for cultivated living."[25] Instead of the over-decorated houses of the day, he advocated for, in a lovely phrase, "unrehearsed experiments of individual designings."[26] But he worried that seeking aesthetic elegance "creates an impossible position, because simplicity for simplicity's sake is as numbing an influence in the creation of art, as ornament for ornament's sake."[27]

Parker and Unwin's essay in Stickley's *The Craftsman* was less concerned with style than with function, convenience, and beauty. They inveighed against an architecture of dead conventions and mourned the fact that the public was principally guided by the expectations of others, therefore getting houses characterized by "meaningless mechanical and superficial ornamentation."[28] It was a grave mistake to bury the structural features of a house in the walls, instead they ought to be exploited for their beauty. In fact, beauty was not something added to the house after it was built but intrinsic to it. If ornament was required, it must be handmade and express the craftsman's pleasure in its making. *The House Beautiful* ran three articles on modern English houses, one of which praised leading English Arts and Crafts architect M. H. Baillie Scott for his "translation of modern aspirations, needs and desires into the concrete."[29]

The English, like Parker and Unwin and the near puritanical Voysey, stressed the necessity of almost radically reforming domestic architecture, insisting that beauty lay in honest structure rather than ornament, and emphasizing simplicity, serenity, and low, horizontal spaces. Massachusetts architects, however, concerned themselves with incorporating the "feeling or spirit of the English country"[30] they found so delightful: hominess, charm, and repose. They seemed to be pursuing the effect of the design on the viewer rather than the revolutionary strategies the English deployed to achieve it.

Given all the attention Americans paid to the English movement, one might find it strange that they were not agreed on what to call it. But one must remember that new styles often receive their names only years after their introduction: in the meantime, it was called simply contemporary or modern. In an illustrated book offering eleven other potential contemporary styles, New York architect Aymar Embury, in 1909, groped to describe an Arts and Crafts house as an "Art Nouveau" house as in a style that "has not yet been named."[31] Believing this new style to be simpler, and therefore better, in America and England than its radically ornamented continental manifestation, he compared the former's "straight lines and plain shapes" to "the self-styled 'craftsman movement,' although without the affectation that mars that work." Unsure as Embury was about how to classify it, he was able to identify the genesis of the unnamed style: "It is mainly by the great English exponents of Art Nouveau, Voysey, Baillie-Scott, and Lutyens, that our modern work has been influenced; and much of it shows a trace of English sentiment. . . ."[32] Strangely, neither Embury nor any of the other commentators thought to call it the Arts and Crafts style.

At least some American critics were selective about the English domestic work that met their approval. As early as 1904, H. Langford Warren undertook a long, well-illustrated piece on the then-contemporary houses in England for *The Architectural Review.* He was adulatory about some of the work, praising the houses of Arts and Crafts architect W. H. Bidlake for qualities that would become bywords for the style: "charming" and "cosy" [sic], as well as others such as "home-like simplicity" and "straightforward expression of simple needs." The review astutely observed other *gemütlich* characteristics: "The low proportions and the small unit of the window openings are essential elements." [33]

If Warren was insightful about the character-defining elements of Arts and Crafts houses, he also responded with mixed feelings, writing of the movement ". . . with all its affectations, with all its straining for novelty, with all its mistakes, (it) has yet undoubtedly done much for the revivification of English handicraft and has produced much genuine and admirable work, especially in the smaller things. . . ." [34] Speaking more particularly and with even greater ambivalence about Voysey, Warren opined, "Among the abler men whom we cannot help but thinking have been somewhat injured by the movement, is Mr. C. F. A. Voysey. His work is well considered and is not without attractiveness, but the sloping buttress-like terminations to the gable ends of his stucco-covered houses, the exaggerated forms of overhanging gables, are notes of affectation which mar otherwise pleasant compositions." [35] Warren was not alone in his somewhat negative evaluation of Arts and Crafts houses, but with time, he was in the minority.

Francis Swales, a Canadian educated in the United States and at the École des Beaux-Arts but practicing architecture in London, used a local journal to ridicule the small English Arts and Crafts houses of England. Not only were they not what Americans would consider well-planned, they were not even convenient or comfortable. To illustrate his point, he charged that most of the houses had no basements or damp-proofing in the floor or walls, lacked bathrooms for the bedrooms and heat in the entrance halls. Because they placed the dining room on one side of the (unheated) entrance hall and the kitchen on the other, serving was inefficient and food cold on arrival. He also disparaged the English custom of providing kitchens with separate sculleries, a practice long abandoned in America. Furthering his contempt, there were no closets in the bedrooms, the houses were poorly heated and with ventilation provided by casement windows—if they opened inward, water would drain on the floor, and if outward, they broke in the wind. Unfortunately, the author somewhat compromised his tirade by admitting that casements were more charming than sash windows and, while they heated rooms better, radiators, beloved by Americans, were "hideous." [36]

Other American critics were markedly more positive. Frank Chouteau Brown, a booster for the Arts and Crafts who practiced, when he could, in the style himself, valued the English movement for "its unpretentiousness, its naiveté and its quiet domesticity."[37] He found English modern houses avoided "the use of conventional architectural forms and moldings, as well as any fixed formality in the balance of façade or use of material."[38] Brown illustrated this concept by describing an Arts and Crafts house that had no conventional cornice and eaves formed only by the projecting rafters, "in the most 'cottagey manner'." Like other critics, Brown prized the English talent for picturesqueness, their "unartificial employment of motif and material and their composition into masses of happily contrasting texture, color and form."[39] He was particularly impressed that in spite of building new houses Lutyens was "consistently picturesque time after time."[40]

However, Brown was perplexed when attempting to define English "modernity of treatment" in English styles like the Arts and Crafts. Giving an only slightly more articulate version of *I know it when I see it*, he averred that such treatment was "easily recognized, (the style) itself so intangible that it is impossible to definitely seize upon and analyze its characteristics—that it is necessary for the American designer to assimilate and to intuitively comprehend before he can even begin to apply its principles in practice. . . ."[41] Here Brown strikingly yokes together two pressing quests—finding a suitable English style to emulate and determining how American architects might then employ it in their own designs.

American critics pointed out two other characteristics of English Arts and Crafts architects they believed to be excellent: the "intense personality and charm of Mr. Voysey's art"[42] and Barry Parker's decision "not to separate the work of the architect from that of the decorator and furnisher. He believes that if a man sets out to design a home he should originate the whole of it."[43] The second observation would certainly apply to Voysey as well.

One must conclude that Massachusetts architects decided to select those elements of English design they believed would fit the needs of their clients or their own design ideals and to ignore those that did not. In plan, architects of the Commonwealth did not break free of convention, eschewing the great hall recommended, if generally not followed, by the English, and preferring the by then standard American living room off a large or small vestibule.

The Development of a New American Style

To promote the acceptance of the Arts and Crafts style in Colonial-identified New England and especially in Massachusetts, the home of the American Revolution, it was necessary for its proponents to make headway against the taste for colonial styles that the American Centennial of 1876 had begun to make popular and newly prestigious. Nostalgia for the past mixed with pride in patriotism cemented American's renewed infatuation with the Colonial, whose very name, ironically, implies a local adaptation of a foreign style.

In 1912, Boston architect J. Lovell Little Jr. felt compelled to deal with the Colonial Revival in a chapter called "The English Modern Plaster House," because he thought it the most serious rival to the English Arts and Crafts style he championed. Although he often designed in the Colonial Revival style himself, he felt the Colonial Revival exemplified "the architecture of a more aristocratic time, . . . of men and women who lived more formally and with less of American independence than we do to-day. It isn't democratic, as we are democratic. . . ."[44] In addition, Colonial Revival houses were more difficult to adapt to newly contemporary requirements of informality.

American proponents of the Arts and Crafts style also had to come to terms with what they believed to be an ethical issue: that of adapting a style of a foreign country, in this case, from England to America. It is ironic that the popular Colonial Revival and Tudor Revival styles were earlier adaptations from the identical country. The simplest tack was to cite the historical fact that America had always "followed at some distance the changing phases of English work down to this time."[45]

F. C. Brown employed the Arts and Crafts dictum of using local materials to justify the American use of plaster, writing that if we use material "near our hands, it rightfully and indisputably belongs to us."[46] In addition, he adopted a somewhat exaggerated economic validation for stucco: because he chose to believe the supply of wood in New England was nearly exhausted and so almost as expensive as stone, brick, or cement, Massachusetts architects were justified in using the cheapest masonry-like material—cementitious stucco.

Like others, Brown worried about the propriety of using non-native American styles. "Our right in America to erect structures in a style copied or derived from that or this or any other period in England is largely a question of ethics."[47] His justification held that "the modern spirit" alone would "legalize"[48] the transportation of traditional forms and motifs from another culture and might perhaps produce something original and personal. Because a truly contemporary solution to ancient problems is "ours by right," we can use it "in precisely the way the English themselves are using it, as a leaven to allow of the incorporation and adaption of Elizabethan or other historical motives into our modern architectural problems."[49] Necessarily, these motifs would have to be adapted to our own purpose and requirements.

Commenting on the growing use by Americans of English historic and current domestic styles, architect Aymar Embury wrote that the resulting styles were "rarely used quite as an English architect would handle them. There is a certain American spirit notable in all which it seems impossible for an architect in the United States to avoid, no matter how deeply he imbues himself in the work of the English past."[50] So even while adopting English styles, Americans could not help being American. The author bolstered the Arts and Crafts authenticity of an American house included in the chapter on the "Modern English" style by stating that it resembled those designed by Voysey but, unlike Voysey, "with his window openings much smaller, reduced in fact, to a size no American owner would permit, largely because of our hotter summers."[51]

Embury went so far in 1909 as to proclaim "Now, at last we have developed rationally and naturally an architectural style which may be fairly called our own."[52] In fact, although he was conflating the eleven styles illustrated in his book, like Brown he was convinced that it was both the modernity of treatment and the subtle adaptations to American conditions that made for a new generalized style. In his chapter on "Modern English," among others, he illustrates three English Arts and Crafts-derived stucco houses, one of which is Charles A. Platt's 36 Amory Street, Brookline, of 1905, (see Figure 2.1) the first of this style in that town. Embury approved of its Colonial Revival door surround as acknowledging its context because he thought Brookline a Colonial town in spite of its preponderance of houses built after the mid-nineteenth century.

Architect Elkin Wallick illustrated, analyzed, priced, and provided building plans for seventeen models of his own design in a book titled *The Small House for a Moderate Income*. He must have thought English-derived Arts and Crafts plans would be popular sellers, as he included at least five in his book, although none under that name. Importantly, he also heralded a new "American Style." His theory ran that modern American architects were eager to break with traditional styles, not so much because they rejected tradition but because they wished to express "something distinctly their own."[53] What they were aiming for above all

FIGURE 2.1 36 Amory Street, Brookline (Charles A. Platt, 1905). The highly detailed, classical door surround suggests the Colonial Revival style, while the proportions and smooth planes of the plain white stucco are Arts and Crafts design elements.

was simplicity without reference to historical ornament, a design that would reflect contemporary living and a limited budget. Wallick did not defend American designs in foreign styles, but simply asserted that we were "justified in claiming them as our own."[54]

American architects were acutely aware that they needed to adapt English Arts and Crafts designs to American tastes and conditions if they were to attract clients. Some, however, were not as concerned about altering English designs for American use as they were unhappy that American architects did not adopt enough authentic English markers of the Arts and Crafts style. For example, architect Allen W. Jackson bemoaned the fact that the average American country house lacked the casement windows, paved terraces, and walled-in stretches of lawn that added hominess to English houses. "To adapt these to our conditions is but the recognition of some sounder building ideas. . . ."[55]

Another impediment to the growth of Arts and Crafts houses lay in Massachusetts residents' predisposition to conventionality. Careful observers of the state's domestic architecture, in comparison with nearby areas such as Providence, Rhode Island, or Portland, Maine, found the houses of Massachusetts were more conservative, understated, and less exuberant than those of similarly populous, historic, and wealthy places. This reticence, with the exception of the most ostentatiously expensive houses, may be a lingering result of the Puritan ethic, but may simply echo the underplayed wealth historically adopted by the state's merchant class.

Frank Chouteau Brown, who came to Massachusetts with fresh eyes from the Midwest, was struck by this characteristic. Going out on a limb for an audience of architects, he stated: "Despite Boston's conventionality, its conservatism—so marked that, it must be confessed, in the greater number of instances it but proclaims itself in a respectable mediocrity. . . ."[56] This was most evident, he thought, in the conservative Bostonian's rejection of stucco: the fact that it may have been cheaper and more up to date than the houses he was accustomed to seeing about him did not influence the risk-averse Bostonian, who preferred to go on reproducing the houses of his predecessors until he realized that he was hopelessly out of date. Perhaps a similarly conformist client had recently rejected the architect's plan to design an Arts and Crafts house when Brown wrote, "When the slightest trace of modern English influence appears sufficient, that is, for him to recognize it as such, the design at once loses its value and appeal."[57]

Another critic, Herbert Crowley, a contributor to the *Architectural Record* from 1891 and its editor from 1900 to 1905, made a similar observation when discussing the contemporary Boston architectural scene: "The atmosphere is not one which encourages originality or any very daring architectural achievement."[58] Perhaps Mary Northland gave the most accurate assessment of the question of style when she described a house by architects Hill and James in Newton (see Figures 2.2a and 2.2b) as being "in a style that

FIGURE 2.2A 47 Windsor Road, Newton (Hill and James, 1907). A long cat-slide roof originally sheltered a porch occupying the last bay on the right. It has been filled in for additional interior space, but the striking massing of the design remains.

might be termed an American development of the English Cottage."[59] Optimistic architects, hoping to create a style that would demonstrate the new technologies and social relationships emerging in the first decades of the twentieth century, believed that Americans had achieved a new, English-inspired Arts and Crafts style. In adapting the English style to our own proclivities, aesthetics, and social expectations, Americans were on the road to a radically simplified look. It would prove to be an excellent fit for the burgeoning suburbs and vacation spots of Massachusetts.

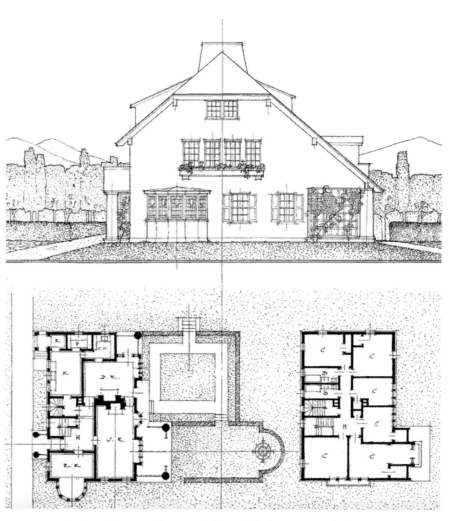

FIGURE 2.2B A plan of the same house as in Figure 2.2a. In a more typical American plan, the kitchen would have been at the rear, but Hill and James reserved the rear rooms for views of the gardens.

1 Neil Swidey, "Trump's Wall and Prescott Hall," *Boston Globe Magazine*, (January 31, 2017), 17–25.

2 H. Langford Warren, "Recent Domestic Architecture in England," *The Architectural Review* XI, no. 1 (January 1904), 5.

3 Allen W. Jackson, "Homes that Architects Have Built for Themselves," *House & Garden* (November 1913), 323, https://archive.org/stream/housegarden23greeuoft/housegarden23greeuoft_djvu.txt.

4 J. Lovell Little Jr, "Modern English Plaster Houses," in Henry Saylor, *Architectural Styles for Country Houses: The Characteristics and Merits of Various Types of Architecture as Set Forth by Enthusiastic Advocates* (New York: McBride, Nast & Co., 1912), 26.

5 Robert Day Andrews, "The Changing Styles of Country Houses," *The Architectural Review* XI, no. 1 (January 1904), 1.

6 Ibid.

7 Arthur G. Bein, "The House and Its Environment: Part I," *The American Architect* XCVII, no. 1776 (January 5, 1910), 5.

8 Herbert Croly, "The Work of Kilham & Hopkins," *The Architectural Record* XXI, no. 2 (February 1912), 97.

9 Frank Chouteau Brown, "Boston Suburban Architecture," *The Architectural Record* 3, no. 4 (April 1907), 252.

10 Reports of the president and the treasurer of Harvard College, 1914–1915, (Cambridge: published by the University, 1916), 131.

11 For example, before going out on their own, Eugene T. Nolte worked for William Rantoul; Parkman B. Haven and Edward H. Hoyt, who would form their own firm, both worked for Edmund Wheelright; and Charles D. Maginnis worked for Peabody and Stearns.

12 In developments of similar or identical houses in Boston, Brookline, and Salem, I enumerate the buildings, not the units.

13 The number is approximate as firm partners combined and recombined. Chapman and Frazer designed fifteen of these houses.

14 "The Joint Exhibition in Boston," *The American Architect* CX, no. 2137 (December 6, 1916), 356.

15 David Gebhard's scholarly article (*Journal of the Society of Architectural Historians* 30, no. 4, (December 1971), 304–312) examined whether Voysey's work in the 1880s, 1890s, and early 1900s "affected American work prior to 1900." However, Gebhard does not stray much beyond the nineteenth century and he is primarily interested in whether Voysey's work was known to the far West and the Midwest's Prairie School. Because I am primarily interested in English-inspired Arts and Crafts houses after 1900, I have not addressed the numerous articles that appeared in journals before that date.

16 "Current Periodicals," *The Architectural Review* 13, no. 12 (January 1906), 12.

17 "Current Periodicals," *The Architectural Review* 10, no. 2 (February 1903), 24.

18 J. H. Elder-Duncan, 1907. *Country Cottages and Weekend Homes* (London: Cassell and Co., Ltd., 1906).

19 Lawrence Weaver, *Small Country Cottages of Today* (London: Country Life, 1910).

20 Henry Saylor, ed., *Architectural Styles for Country Houses: The Characteristics and Merits of Various Types of Architecture as Set Forth by Enthusiastic Advocates* (New York: McBride, Nast & Co., 1912).

21 Ekin Wallick, *The Small House for a Moderate Income* (New York: Hearst's International Library Co., Inc., 1915), 11.

22 Ibid., 13–14.

23 Charles Holme, ed., "Modern British Domestic Architecture and Decoration," *The Studio* (London, Paris, New York: 1901), 3.

24 Edward S. Prior, "The Movement of English Architecture," *The Architectural Review* New Series 5, no. 2 (February 1909), 43.

25 Ibid., 44.

26 Ibid.

27 Ibid.

28 Barry Parker and Raymond Unwin, "The Art of Building a Home," in Gustav Stickley, *Craftsman Homes* (New York: Craftsman Publishing Company, 1909), 7.

29 Edward Gregory, "The Architecture of the Modern English Home: The Work of Mr. M. H. Baillie Scott," *House Beautiful* (August 1911), 67.

30 Frank Chouteau Brown, "Suburban Homes," *Good Housekeeping* 38, no. 4 (October 1903), 302.

31 Aymar Embury II, *One Hundred Country Houses: Modern American Examples* (New York: The Century Co., 1909), 194.

32 Ibid., 196.

33 Warren H. Langston, "Recent Domestic Architecture in England," *The Architectural Review* 11, no. 1 (January 1904), 11.

34 Ibid., 12. By "smaller things" Warren probably meant smaller houses rather than handicrafts.

35 Ibid.

36 Francis S. Swales. "The Small English Home as a Place to Live In—Its Seamy Side," *The Architectural Record* XXV, no. 6 (June 1909), 403.

37 Frank Chouteau Brown, "The Relationship Between English and American Domestic Architecture," *The Brickbuilder* 15, no. 9 (September 1906), 189.

38 Ibid.

39 Ibid., 191.

40 Ibid., 190.

41 Ibid.

42 "Current Periodicals," *The Architectural Review* 12, no. 5 (May 1903), 60.

43 Edward W. Gregory, "Architects of the Modern English Home: The Work of Mr. R. Barry Parker," *The House Beautiful* 30, no. 4 (September 1911), 117.

44 J. Lovell Little Jr., "Modern English Plaster Houses," 28.

45 H. Langford Warren, "Recent Domestic Architecture in England," *The Architectural Review* (January 1904), 12.

46 Frank Chouteau Brown, "The Relation Between English and American Domestic Architecture: The Influence of Materials," *The Brickbuilder* 15, no. 8 (August 1906), 160.

47 Ibid., 161

48 Ibid., 162.

49 Ibid., 158.

50 Aymar Embury II, *One Hundred Country Houses*, 152.

51 Ibid., 164.

52 Ibid., 7.

53 Ekin Wallick, *The Small House for a Moderate Income*, 43

54 Ibid., 44.

55 Allen W. Jackson, "Homes That Architects Build for Themselves," 295.

56 Frank Chouteau Brown, "Boston Suburban Architecture," *The Architectural Record* (April 1907), 254.

57 Ibid., 258–259.

58 Herbert Croly, "The Work of Kilham & Hopkins," *The Architectural Record* XXI, no. 2 (February 1912), 98. Croly went on to become an important public intellectual in the Progressive movement, cofounder of *The New Republic*, and the author of seminal books that influenced Teddy Roosevelt and later the New Deal.

59 Mary H. Northland, "The Interesting Stucco House of W. C. Strong, Esq., at Waban, Massachusetts," *American Homes and Gardens* (October 1909), 386.

Chapter Three
ARTS AND CRAFTS HOUSES FOR THE MASSACHUSETTS SUBURBS

*I*n 1906, the editors of Boston's *The Architectural Review* asked their subscribers to provide ideas for future articles. They were not surprised to find that the most attractive of any subject was the design of modest houses—"The small dwelling . . . the sort of house which is now being built by the thousands in the suburbs of our larger cities and in the smaller towns as well."[1] One can see why it was such a popular topic. The explosion of suburban construction placed local architects in a position of having to create a previously unthinkable number of individual houses, each different but, in conservative Massachusetts, not so exceptionally different as to flout the existing normative idea of "home." Indeed, Ekin Wallick stated that he published his 1915 book of plans and elevations, *The Small House for a Moderate Income*, due to "The rapid development of suburban tracts of land in almost every part of the country has created a widespread demand for good houses of intelligent design, planned with an ideal of comfort and convenience as well as artistic merit."[2]

⁙ The Forces for Suburbanization ⁙

The upsurge in suburban construction in Massachusetts in the first two decades of the twentieth century was due to several factors that stemmed from the late nineteenth century. Massachusetts was growing significantly more urbanized and its cities were attracting new and often impoverished immigrants. Concurrently, a growing, newly moneyed upper middle class—lawyers, bankers, company executives, and the like—wished to surround their families with those of similar economic status and had the resources to commission suburban houses from local architects, purchase ready-made plans, or buy a house on speculation. The move from the noisy, crowded city to the quiet, safe, and green openness of the suburbs made an attractive option for those who could afford it. No wonder clients and architects alike were hungry for information about house styles, plans, and materials suited to suburban lots.

The stucco Arts and Crafts house in Massachusetts is primarily a product of this suburbanization. City cores were already built up, with few nearby lots available for purchase unless a landowner opened his acres for development within city limits. Several stucco houses were built as seasonal homes in seaside settings and a few others as country houses for year-round living, but most were found in growing suburbs where vacant land and good transportation offered an appealing choice. For example, Brookline, a Boston suburb, retains thirty relatively unaltered Arts and

Crafts houses, the largest collection in the state. The town grew from a population of 23,436 in 1905 to 37,748 in 1920, an astounding 61 percent growth. Similarly situated Newton, with twenty-one Arts and Crafts houses, grew in the same period by 25 percent; Winchester, which has eleven significant Arts and Crafts houses, by 27 percent, and Longmeadow, a well-to-do suburb of Springfield, grew by what must have been an alarming 70 percent.

Several factors contributed to the lure of the suburbs. In Brookline, the renowned architect and planning firm of Olmsted and Olmsted improved streetscapes by laying out five sensitively designed residential subdivisions with distinctive curving streets. The firm also redesigned and engineered such major streets as Beacon, Chestnut, and Boylston. The socially exclusive Country Club of Brookline opened in 1882 on one hundred acres. An authority on American suburbs believed the club, "was one of the primary agencies for preserving the cohesiveness of Boston society and making suburban residence the social equal of the older neighborhoods."[3] Water, sewer, and electric public utilities developed in each suburb at different times, but they arrived in almost all the suburbs included here before 1900. These public services were seldom inducements to move, but potential residents might have resisted moving beyond the city had they had not existed. Because Newton often connected a new house to its water system before the Town required building permits, often the only method of dating a house is by finding a penciled entry noting the day it was connected to town water in field books kept by the Water Department.

The development of Boston suburbs, a phenomenon that began in earnest only in the late 1840s, was, not surprisingly, driven by transportation methods and the infrastructure they used. According to James C. O'Connell, the historian of Boston's metropolis, no Boston suburbs existed before 1820. Previously, people of means used the city's borderlands as sites for vacation houses, not for permanent residences. Railroad suburbs began to prosper from the 1840s when freight trains started carrying commuters as well as goods: after 1870, streetcar suburbs followed streetcar lines into a countryside dotted with small, traditional village centers. The Metropolitan Parkway system (1895–1945) and other new paved roads led automobiles to house sites in the formerly inaccessible interstices between streetcar or rail tracks, or yet farther afield to outlying villages.

For commuters, the bucolic and quiet house site, affordability of the land, suitability of the house, and complexion of the neighborhood would be as nothing without efficient access to transportation to one's job in the city. Train service was the first to carry commuters from home to work in Boston and back. Brookline had service by the 1830s, Winchester and Newton followed in the 1840s. Most suburban lines undertook improvements that greatly increased capacity in the 1870s and mid-1880s, making their destinations increasingly viable as places of residence. The Boston and Albany Railroad employed the renowned architect H. H. Richardson to design several elegant railroad stations in Newton and hired the prestigious Olmsted's firm to landscape them. If suburban dwellers had to travel to Boston for work or recreation, their arrivals and departures could be accomplished with style.

The descriptive phrase, "streetcar suburb" was coined in 1969 by the perceptive Boston University scholar Sam Bass Warner, but it was a fact on the ground long before. By 1856, Cambridge had horse-drawn streetcar service and by 1868, Newton followed. In 1889, the West End rail line electrified the streetcars whose lines had webbed Greater Boston, with greatly expanded service in 1895. A historian writing in 1905 described the effect of better commuting options in Newton, which, until the turn of the century, had been composed of several scattered villages. "The ever-increasing waves of population moving out into the suburban zones of Greater Boston have long ago filled in the spaces between the older villages of Newton and built up new settlements at some distances to the railway stations. The development of electric tram-lines, of which this suburb has an admirable system, has aided this. . . ." [4] The author goes on to say the "cheapness" of transportation, the ease of access to the resources of the city, as well as the "reasonable land," were selling points for Newton commuters.

Aside from fully designed subdivisions, the eventual suburban development patterns—road shape, size, and destinations; town centers; house lots; and transportation nodes—were the outcome of a multitude of individual deci-sions rather than cohesively planned results. This is not the place to examine the aesthetics, quality, or shape of these suburbs, or even that of individual house lots, but we must remember that these suburbs were created by transportation executives, real estate agents, and sellers' and buyers' vision of what constituted the ideal domestic environment, limited only by the income of those wishing, or resigned, to reside there.

For example, developers laid out smaller lots near railroad stations or streetcar stops and larger, and therefore more expensive ones, farther from the noise of the cars. "Brookline represented a social winnowing that took place as each suburb established its socioeconomic niche." [5] By the 1880s it became known as the richest town in the world. To maintain class distinctions, the earlier and wealthier settlers tended to control development. Those in charge provided city services to large houses on large lots and reduced their tax assessment, while small houses on small lots were lucky to get access roads and were the last to receive town services.

The single-family house set back behind a well-kept lawn as part of a streetscape of similar dwellings in a continuous green frontage became the stereotypical image of the suburb. Some attribute this iconic image to the distinguished landscape designer Frederick Law Olmsted and his firm. Olmsted may have romanticized the landscape, but in such suburbs as Newton, the organized development of substantial houses and their lawns laid out around an ar-

FIGURE 3.1A Sunset Rock, 20 Eastern Point Boulevard, Gloucester (architect unknown, 1914). The approach to the house creates for the visitor an unfolding drama and a sense of the power of nature.

FIGURE 3.1B Sunset Rock, 20 Eastern Point Boulevard, Gloucester, Massachusetts. Further along the private road the house begins to be revealed.

chitect-designed park were present as early as 1845. A few sophisticated Arts and Crafts architects and their clients sometimes allowed themselves to break from the cultural norm of the green front yard by deploying distinctive landscape characteristics such as massive, romantic rock outcroppings or steep hills to become the significant feature. This was true of the 1908 suburban house at 15 Hobart Terrace, Newton, by Edmund Q. Sylvester, with later additions. Perched high on a hill overlooking dramatic rock outcrop-

pings behind the house, a discriminating critic was struck by the way the architect adapted the design "to the rough and broken character of the natural surroundings, and proves how much can be done by means of the free and vigorous handling of motifs, which are popular in this country and usually commonplace in their effect."[6]

An even more dramatic use of rocks occurs in a vacation house, aptly named "Sunset Rock," above an ocean beach in Gloucester. Huge exposed boulders in the front

FIGURE 3.1C The unknown architect used the site in an exclusive area to great effect for this rustic but comfortable seaside vacation home.

lawn and the nearly hidden dome of a high-perched garden pavilion provide an impressive contrast between the natural and man-made for the visitor approaching the house (see Figure 3.1a). Farther along the road a sliver of the house is almost teasingly revealed behind the powerful granite display (see Figure 3.1b). Only when reaching a break in the long fieldstone wall defining the property does the house come into full view with its prominent fieldstone porch and sunroom (see Figure 3.1c). The use of these stones in the fabric of the house effectively unites it with the landscape from which they were taken.

❧ Site and Orientation ☙

Sir Lawrence Weaver's book on small country houses identified an important design issue: "Suburban houses built on small plots of land create problems of planning which are absent from country houses where sites are not only larger but more widely spaced."[7] The American architect Elkin Wallace addressed this issue when he said of his own design for "An American Home in the English Style," "To be sure, the exterior treatment of this house is more distinctly English than the plan, but few of our building sites have the proper surroundings to enable us to use the English plan as it is found in English country houses."[8] In effect, architect-designed country houses for wealthy English clients simply would not fit on our more limited suburban sites.

While the English valued privacy above all, setting the house as far from the public way as possible and hiding it behind courtyards and high hedges, Americans actively wanted to display the façade of their houses. Architect J. Lovell Little Jr. complained, "In this country, the suburban house is as much for the public as for the owner. . . . Each man tries to outdo his neighbor in the smoothness of his lawn and in the display of shrubs and flower beds, an effort that gives no adequate return in comfort or beauty."[9] Similarly, the judges of a 1917 competition for the design of small, single family houses, determined the best method of achieving their aim of "livability" was to turn the face of the house to the garden rather than the street. They admitted, however, that in taking this position they were ignoring "a well-known fact of American psychology"[10] that American men and women were so enamored of the life of the street that they were willing to sacrifice their privacy.

The primacy of the garden dictated in part the location of the major rooms of the English house, so that the living and dining rooms faced a green and private space in the most secluded part of the lot. In contrast, Americans almost invariably placed these rooms at the front. Wallick described Americans as feeling the English model not only impractical but essentially crazy. In America, "The idea of placing the kitchen on the front of the house, so that the living room and dining room may face the garden is considered insane. . . ."[11]

Charles A. Platt, a New York architect who ordinarily designed country houses in an Italianate style for the very wealthy, authored an article in a 1906 issue of *Indoors and*

Out on his Arts and Crafts house for Henry Howard, an MIT graduate, chemical company executive, and a director of the Boston Dwelling House Company (see Figure 2.1). He argued, "To successfully plan a suburban property is to plan the ground as well as the house. It is only by unifying these that every foot of space can be utilized."[12] In contrast to conventional American siting practice, Platt turned back from the dusty street to place the principle rooms opening onto a verandah at the rear and garden beyond. This meant that the kitchen was located in the basement, an arrangement made possible by plentiful servants.

In this compact design, Platt placed a poured concrete garage at a walkout basement level: his accommodation of the car within the main body of the dwelling, was the first in Brookline and a rare use in English-inspired Arts and Crafts houses. Other architects, caring less about preserving room for a fine garden on small, suburban lots, built "auto houses" as separate or semidetached structures. Platt took much pride in his accomplishment in Brookline:

"Limited space at command here produced vertical lines; and the lofty proportioned house we see, bound to its suburban site as it is by a harmonious fence, has all the charms of the best modern English or Scotch cottages."[13] At the rear he laid out flowerbeds and walks, and provided a roomy veranda facing the garden, itself screened from neighbors by trellises and trees. To make the house sparkle, Platt added to the stucco's final coat a "finely ground silica which causes the beautiful white surface distinguishing the house."[14]

The extraordinary expansion of the suburbs after the turn of the twentieth century by homeowners wealthy enough to hire an architect provided designers enough scope to try out a style imported from England but shaped by American lot sizes, mores, aesthetic preferences, climate, and available materials. Massachusetts architects would learn much from English architects but perhaps even more from each other as they faced the challenges of creating the modern suburban house. In attempting to meet this goal they created a distinctive American style.

❧ Notes ❧

1 Publisher's Department, *The Architectural Review* XVII, no. III (February 1906), vii.

2 Ekin Wallick, *The Small House for a Moderate Income*, 11.

3 Kenneth Jackson, *Crabgrass Frontier: The Suburbanization of the United States* (New York: Oxford University Press, 1985), 98.

4 John Wescott. "The Newtons II: A Mature American Suburb," *Indoors and Out* 1, no. 2 (November 1905), 77.

5 James C. O'Connell. *The Hub's Metropolis: Greater Boston's Development from Railroad Suburb to Smarth Growth* (Cambridge: MIT Press, 2013), 48.

6 "The Small Country House: A Collection of Impressive but Well-Designed Suburban Dwellings," *The Architectural Record* 28, no. 3 (September 1910), 282.

7 Sir Lawrence Weaver, *Small Country Houses of To-day*, Vol. I (London: *Country Life* and New York: Scribner, 3rd ed., 1922), 118.

8 Ekin Wallick, *The Small House for a Moderate Income*, 34.

9 J. Lovell Little Jr., *Indoors and Out* (January 1906), 191.

10 National Fire Proofing Co., "Competition for a One-Family House: Report of the Jury of Award," *The NATCO Tex-Tile One Family House* (Boston: Rogers and Mason, 1917), 7.

11 Ekin Wallick, *The Small House for a Moderate Income*. 53.

12 Charles A. Platt, "A Cement House Containing a Garage," *Indoors and Out* III, no. 3 (December 1906), 123.

13 Ibid., 126.

14 Ibid. The house has recently been painted without the sparkly silica addition.

In the first two decades of the twentieth century, British architectural critics discussed Arts and Crafts as a movement rather than a style. This seemed appropriate because English and Scottish architects who dealt with domestic architecture produced such very different work; their houses had little in common but an attitude, a vague sense of pared-down newness, and the period during which they were built. Although it is notoriously difficult to describe or pin down, I have chosen, as the simplest way to describe this complex phenomenon, to refer to the English-inspired Arts and Crafts domestic work in Massachusetts as a style. These houses share a wide palette of architectural gestures adopted from English examples but translated into the aesthetics, environmental needs, site requirements, available materials, and preferences of the architects and owners who built them. What follows is an illustrated description of these features.

⁜ Stucco: The Uniting Characteristic ⁜

The one element that united a considerable number of Massachusetts Arts and Crafts houses was the choice of stucco as a building material. Because nearly all the English houses that inspired Massachusetts domestic architecture were constructed in brick or stone, it was important for Massachusetts architects to produce an image that spoke of masonry. But brick and stone were costly in a state that had little inexpensive local stone and lacked a sufficient supply of skilled stonemasons.[1] Stucco, which could be applied as an exterior finish coat to a base of wood framing with supporting wood or metal lathing, concrete, or terra cotta block, became a handy stand-in. An ancient material, known to the Egyptians and Romans, stucco was the common protective skin in the missions of early California and in Spanish-controlled Florida. Stucco was also used in the early nineteenth century in Regency architecture in England and in Federal buildings in the United States, and so became well known to American architects who studied significant works of the past.

Historically, stucco was composed of natural materials: hydrated or slaked lime, water, and sand, to which was added binding materials such as straw or animal hair. Portland cement, by contrast, developed in England in the 1820s and improved thereafter, was composed of heated clay and limestone that hardened with the addition of water. In the early twentieth century stucco made with artificial Portland cement and lime gained popularity because the introduction of cheaper, American-manufactured cement, made it easier to work, more durable and more widely available.

When, after 1900, stucco became popular all over the country for the exteriors of Mission and Spanish Colonial style houses, it recalled a romantic, almost mythic past. Frank Lloyd Wright and Prairie School architects, practicing a distinctly midwestern brand of Arts and Crafts, used stucco to highlight the simple planes that set off the striking horizontal massing of their then very modern houses. Massachusetts architects found the warmth and simplicity of stucco's surfaces could be used at advantage for their English-derived Arts and Crafts houses.

According to the *Brick and Clay Record*, a violently anti-stucco trade publication for brickmakers and workers, stucco experienced a "craze" in the early twentieth century.[2] The *Bulletin* of the Building Trades Employers' Association stated in 1909, "there is no material for the decoration of both the exterior and interior of houses that had undergone more of a revival during the last few years than stucco. . . . Day by day its popularity is increasing."[3] The home shelter periodical, *Keith's Magazine*, endorsed the material because "there is good reason for its popularity."[4] With its use, fire resistance could be had at little increase in cost, it was pleasing for aesthetic reasons, and, possibly as important, it satisfied home buyers' desire for "something different."[5] By 1916, some said that stucco's very success had become a source of its diminished reputation: "Modern competition has made a serious inroad on the popularity of stucco . . . as

FIGURE 4.1 Clinton Wire Lath Co. advertisement. This building material ad, aimed at homeowners rather than architects, has the architect promoting stucco's ease of maintenance and structural reliability: "Yes Madam, the stucco house I am building for you will be beautiful, but what is of greater importance, it will have permanence and freedom from repairs, for I have specified Clinton Wire Lath to support the stucco."

it has caused workmen to be forced to adopt cheap and inferior methods in mixing and applying the work."[6] However, with the addition of a waterproofing agent stucco became more impervious to rain and damp, while the availability of inexpensive, easy to install metal and wire lath substantially replaced the traditional but flammable split-wood lath used as a foundation for stucco. (See Figure 4.1.) Since the Arts and Crafts movement was a reaction to the Queen Anne style's fascination with complicated asymmetry, irregular shapes, and elaborate decorative trim, the smooth, nearly monotone stucco was a natural antidote. Frank Chouteau Brown voiced an aesthetic reason for appreciating stucco: "The very solidity of the material results in an architectural style of less finical restlessness of appearance than the use of the more easily worked wood allows."[7] In other words, it was so easy to create a fussy design in wood and so difficult to do so in stucco that the result was inevitably quieter. Similarly, an article titled "The Value of Stucco" in a 1919 issue of *The House Beautiful*, claimed that masonry contributed to the significance of the design "for the economical building of masonry requires large and simple masses and few openings. . . . when such restrictions are put upon the builder he will study carefully the position of the openings of his walls and group them where they most serve the needs of the occupant."[8]

The architects who coated their houses with stucco intended to achieve the appearance of stone or concrete. To convey this impression, instead of the flat horizontal lintel, standard in wood-frame houses for window, door, or porch openings, they often employed the shallow segmental or three-centered arch most efficient in masonry construction. (See Figures 4.4, 4.36, and 4.32.) Color is one of the first things viewers notice about a house. The English architect C. F. A. Voysey whitewashed his roughcast (a more heavily textured stucco) a brilliant white, as if to make his handmade houses stand out from their natural surroundings. (See Figures 1.2, 1.3, and 1.4.) Massachusetts architects tended to prefer colors that mimicked stone—pale grays and yellows and earth tones, though many opted for white or cream. Stucco only needs painting when deteriorated so getting the original color right was and continues to be important. I have generally made stucco a required gesture for inclusion in this study, but I have no difficulty in breaking this rule if a house displays enough other Arts and Crafts architectural imagery to make it a good candidate.

What Is an Arts and Crafts House?

The following five houses will help to define the question "What is a Massachusetts Arts and Crafts House?" None of these examples will by themselves provide an answer, but as a group they show something of the style's variety and fancifulness, the multiple uses of an architectural gesture, and the sense of the newness they display. The five can be further divided into two groups: the fresh, bold, almost radically a-historic quality of the first two examples, and the quaint, cozy, English Cottage imagery of the last three. Nonetheless,

FIGURE 4.2 1547 Centre Street, Newton (Robert Coit, 1912). Set on a rise, the house combines local Arts and Crafts motifs: the dramatic roof, tile ornament, buttressed entry and integrated porch. The shallow segmental arch of the porch appears in masonry houses such as this and repeated by others in the more usual stucco over wood.

FIGURE 4.3 30 Maplewood Terrace, Springfield (architect unknown, 1912). The exaggerated diagonal of the battered or buttressed wall juxtaposed with the forceful curve of the roof and the robust Craftsman-style entry combine to make a strong statement.

FIGURE 4.4 42 Waterston Road, Newton (Chapman and Frazer, 1909). Contributing to soften the fortress-like character of this subtle house are the clipped or jerkin-head roofs and gentle segmental arch of the entry porch, while the leaded glass windows and window boxes add to the picturesque effect.

FIGURE 4.5 202 Brattle Street, Cambridge (Allen W. Jackson, 1903). Battered brick walls and the Tudor arch of the garage lend a humor and whimsicality not seen in most Arts and Crafts houses. The major rooms face south on an extensive garden or west on a public park.

FIGURE 4.6 59 Holland Road, Brookline (Chapman and Frazer, 1915). Set on the downslope of a hill, the house is in cozy contact with the ground in front while an elevated porch at the rear overlooks a distant view. The jetty overhang emphasizes the horizontal line.

FIGURE 4.6A 59 Holland Road, Brookline (Chapman and Frazer, 1915). These exterior benches suggest comfort, ease, and companionship even before one enters the house.

even in the first group, closer analysis of a Newton house by architect Robert Coit, displays historicizing multigabled and catslide roofs found in centuries-old English vernacular houses (see Figure 4.2). Its construction of hollow terra cotta tile covered in stucco was unusual for architect-designed upper-middle-class houses, although it was also used in a group of workers' houses described in Chapter 5.

The remarkable house in Springfield (see Figure 4.3), with its absence of cornices and moldings and the clean lines enhanced by smooth stucco, also looks starkly modern. However, it also carries a distinctive curved eaves line reminiscent of an English thatched roof, and dramatic flaring buttresses that might once have supported the walls of an ancient British stone manor house or castle.

Similarly, the second, more picturesque group, empha-

sized charm and a pronounced "olde" English heritage, but all three also display a quirky modernity that critics of the day had such a problem defining. In 1912, *American Homes and Gardens* described this house in Newton (see Figure 4.4) by Chapman and Frazer as having a second-story overhang "in imitation of seventeenth century homes, and the deep pitched roof also suggests Colonial influence."[9] It also stated that the stucco served to "emphasize the quaintness of the whole."[10] But the severe horizontality emphasized by the jettied second story, non-symmetrical façade, and entry with battered walls makes the design seem almost modern.

Designed as the architect Allen W. Jackson's own dwelling, the 1903 house on Cambridge's elegant Brattle Street (see Figure 4.5) is certainly striving for a nostalgic look. Jackson considered that, "aside from the plan . . . the house was inspired by the contemporary work as it is being done in England for those who have sought out the quiet mellowness of the little villages."[11] Indeed, it combines so many historic English features that it appears he was using the house as a catalogue of his ability to treat them in novel ways. Included are the staggered roofline with high-pitched roof, catslide roof, and jettied or overhanging second floor. Add to this list the banked windows, which can be casements filled with bull's eye or leaded glass diamond-paned lights, as well as buttresses at the rear. The entrance to the garage, placed daringly for the period on the façade, contains a brick Tudor arched opening flanked by stubby buttresses, surmounted by a half-timber gable with a leaded glass window. On the other hand, the house looks neither like an ancient dwelling transported from an English village nor a comfortable-looking Arts and Crafts house by an English architect. It is a quirky American blend of both.

The last house in this second group (see Figure 4.6), by the prolific architect Horace S. Frazer of the firm Chapman and Frazer, repeats the second-floor overhang, but softens the composition with the wavy line of the eaves meant to suggest a thatched roof. Banded casements and an oriel window on the left add to the picturesque quality of the whole. The least modern of the five examples, the snug built-in benches sheltered by a substantial canopy and the heart-shaped cutouts in the first-floor shutters make a claim for old-fashioned hominess (see Figure 4.6a).

⁌ Relationship to the Ground ⁌

One of the features American architects admired about English vernacular houses was their intimate relationship to the ground. From an American point of view, "In most instances one enters the English house practically on the ground level, which adds an indefinable charm, and still we continue to raise our houses four or five steps off the ground, which, in many cases, tends to ruin the general proportions . . . by pushing the whole house up into the air."[12] A nearly identical complaint by an author of a book on model houses held that "The charm of the English cottage lies largely in their tile or thatch roofs and low stories set close to the ground, all of which in this country we must abandon at their outset. . . ."[13] Architect James Hopkins of Kilham & Hopkins commended the English habit of siting their houses low for "knitting man's work and nature's into the most intimate relations."[14] And Allen W. Jackson went so far as to recommend fitting the American house to uneven ground "by lowering or raising the floor level with changes in grade."[15]

Many upper-class English houses provided storage and work space in a series of small rooms behind the kitchen, but in Massachusetts, homeowners required a windowed basement for their furnaces and the coal they burned, their seasonal sports equipment and lawn furniture and their oversized travel trunks. High foundation walls were needed to provide the headroom and basement windows required for these underground spaces, provoking the above complaints. The tall foundations may have made Massachusetts dwellings more imposing or even stately, but at the expense of some hominess.

A house by Thomas Mott Shaw (see Figure 4.7), set with its façade perpendicular to the street, sits snuggly on its site, increasing the approachability it lost by turning its side to the road.[16] At another Brookline site, J. Lovell Little Jr. used the descending slope of the lot to "place the front directly on the ground, giving an easy step from the walk to the front porch. The house is thus saved from being perched up in the air in stilted fashion."[17] The grade change also allowed cellar windows to be placed on the sides and rear rather than the front (see Figure 4.45). Approximately one quarter of the houses selected for this book display low foundations.

FIGURE 4.7 7 Pine Road, Brookline (Thomas Mott Shaw, 1916). A popular trope was the use of two prominent gables, here with a catslide roofs. The house is only one step up from ground level. (See also Figures 4.24, 4.32, and 4.36.)

⊰ Plan ⊱

English Arts and Crafts country houses tended to spread out on the landscape with courtyards, wings, and terraces, but a house on a small Massachusetts suburban lot generally had no such options as compactness was required. The size and shape of a suburban lot naturally had a critical effect on the internal planning of the house created for it. For example, speaking of designing for a row of narrow lots, Frank Chouteau Brown wrote "In such cases the frontage is small, and the first difficulty arises out of the hall. We recognize that to make it a sort of narrow passage is a mistake...some fair-sized space must be allowed if the house is to be satisfactory."[18] This is probably why the architects of several Arts and Crafts houses on narrow lots placed the shorter side parallel to the street so the longer side could contain a center entry with roomy center hall, so standard to the American Colonial Revival plan (see Figures 4.7 and 4.42).

Cultural attitudes have much to do with creating the plan of a home. In comparing the distinction between the English love of privacy and the American's desire for openness, J. Lovell Little Jr. wrote of the English ". . . one goes from room to room without being able to see more than a few feet ahead. . . ."[19] However, in the United States, "one room often opens widely into another or into the hall and the family group around the living room fireplace can be seen from almost any point on the first floor."[20] Similarly, architect Frank Chouteau Brown, complained that in the English suburban house "Each room is considered by itself and with little regard to unity of scheme in the whole interior. . . ."[21] Ironically, and very much to the point, he continued, while the arrangement of rooms in English country houses was haphazard, "the rooms being placed just where they are wanted, with little thought of design in their placing, is in part undoubtedly productive of that picturesqueness which we admire."[22] Allen Jackson attributed American rejection of privacy in house planning to a feeling that privacy itself was somehow "snobbish and unfriendly, perhaps a trifle undemocratic. . . ."[23]

At the turn of the century, American attitudes towards privacy were in flux. Family life was becoming less formal and less hierarchical, with more openness and fewer servants. A house plan that rigidly divided space into a parlor or receiving room for guests and a small living room for the family was no longer a social necessity. Said architect J. Lovell Little Jr., "All this makes for a new type of house . . . with at least one large living room that typifies the life of the household."[24] This new simplification, openness of plan, and personal interaction was made possible in part by the introduction at the end of the nineteenth century of a technical improvement—coal-fired central heating. Consequently, closed doors were no longer required to retain the heat from a stove or open fire, making fireplaces function as a point for social gathering rather than warmth.

The English Arts and Crafts house shape was ideally supposed to result from the placement of rooms in relations to the site features, view, sun, and ventilation rather than symmetry. But partly due to the New England predilection for formal Colonial and Federal planning, Massachusetts homebuyers preferred a central entry hall off which the principal public rooms opened. This formalism

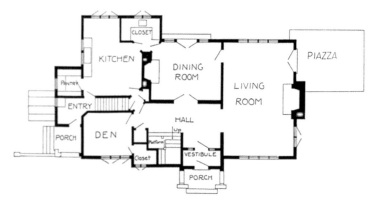

FIGURE 4.8 Plan, 42 Waterston Road, Newton (see Figure 4.4). The meaning of the term "center hall" is shown in this plan where the hall gives onto to every ground floor room except the kitchen. Massachusetts architects believed their clients valued openness over both privacy and mystery, but note the interior doors that allowed the dining room and den to be closed off if desired.

may have caused Massachusetts Arts and Crafts architects to be conflicted between the need to accommodate their clients' desire for a central hall and their own desire for the picturesque English model of seemingly haphazardly but happily placed rooms. The caption for Figure 4.36 catches the English expectation that "whether symmetrical or not, the English plaster type of exterior grows naturally from the floor plan."[25]

The American center hall, or quasi-center hall arrangement did not strictly require replicating the organization of the façade on either side of the front entry, but it often resulted in a somewhat symmetrical, or, as in Figure 4.8, a carefully balanced façade. (See Figure 4.4 for the exterior

of this house.) Fortunately, symmetry could be disguised by several strategies. Among them were offset dormers; staggering front rooms to break up the façade; different window types or groupings; and adding a large exterior chimney at the façade. Indeed, the author of a description of a Chapman and Frazer house in Newton with a center hall plan described as "a good example of an American adaptation of the modern English type cottage" was almost apologetic when he stated that while it is "more symmetrical than its prototypes it is by no means stiff or severe."[26] (See Figure 4.49.)

We have noted American criticism of the remoteness of English kitchens from the dining room, although this must have applied only to the larger houses. Americans tended to deal with the nearness of the two by substituting for distance, a small butler's pantry with a closing door to the dining room. The word for this space was clearly adopted from English precedent although it would be highly unusual for the owners of nearly all the houses discussed here to employ a butler. In New England it was also called a china closet or serving pantry.[27] Massachusetts architects complained about the space-wasting, inefficient English kitchen itself, especially "given the servant problem in this country."[28] They also increasingly rejected as "extremely impractical"[29] the English division of the cooking area into separate rooms for the kitchen (food preparation and stove), larder (food storage), and scullery (washing up) often strung out in an ell. Instead, Americans tended to combine these functions in one space and by efficiency of design, reduce the size of the kitchen, probably because, as the twentieth century progressed, middle-class homes had fewer servants.

By 1913, a modern kitchen would have had generous counter space—a relatively new amenity; top and bottom cabinets; a sink with running water; built-in breadboard and bread kneading tray; coal and gas ranges side by side, and a hot water boiler. The icebox was frequently placed in a porch with a door to the outside so the iceman could remove an old ice block and insert a new one without entering the house. Water from leaking ice would be kept out of the kitchen as well. Bathrooms in the early twentieth century tended to be regarded as expensive and space-wasting, as seen in an architect's advice to prospective homeowners in 1913 to supply the master bedroom with its own bathroom while the other family members would probably have to share. Often, one bathroom served the whole family. Equally, multiple bedroom closets were not obvious requirements: the same architect suggested, as if an unusual idea, that each person ought to have one closet which should be supplied with poles for coat hangers, the large wardrobe as the sole place for storing hanging clothing having slipped out of fashion.

⊰ Shape ⊱

Massachusetts Arts and Crafts houses were designed in a variety of shapes: about one half were approximately rectangu-lar and a third of these had one or more ells. A fine example of a compact rectangular house was erected in Cambridge in 1910 by architect C. H. Bartlett (see Figure 4.9). Its strong geometric shape is only slightly softened on the façade by a center entry portico flanked by bow and bay windows. An example of more linear house form is the Tudor-inflected house in Gloucester (see Figure 4.10). Although not as starkly rectilinear as Voysey's Perrycroft's garden elevation, it shares the long massing and deep hip roof (see Figure 1.2). Another group of houses assumed more complex forms that can be described by letters of the alphabet such as T, H, L, and a splayed U. The 1909 house that architect Thomas Mott Shaw designed in Concord on a large piece of property for his own residence is arranged with the open arms of the U defining an entry court on the façade (see Figure 4.11), more usual in English than Massachusetts practice.[30] The house at 219 Buckminster Road, Brookline (see Figure 4.12), employs a similar splayed U shape in response to its site on a rounded corner of a modest suburban lot.

⊰ Massing ⊱

The architectural term "massing" suggests a three-dimensional expression of shape and the space that a building encloses, as well as the human experience of looking. Its meaning thus includes not only raw shape, size, and proportion but also the elements that affect one's perception of them. Over half of the houses in this study are two-and-one-half stories high, about forty percent are two stories high, and roughly

FIGURE 4.9 117 Lake View Avenue, Cambridge (C. H. Bartlett, 1910). The strong outline of the deeply overhanging, lid-like roof emphasizes the dwelling's rectangular shape.

FIGURE 4.10 20 Souther Road, Gloucester (architect unknown, ca. 1903–1916). A string course in a contrasting color reinforces the horizontal lines of the jetty and the banked windows.

FIGURE 4.11 345 Garfield Road, Concord (Thomas Mott Shaw, 1909). Shaw, having studied architecture in France, was drawn to the formality of French planning, including a main block with wings ending in dependencies or pavilions. The picture window is a later alteration.

FIGURE 4.12 219 Buckminster Road, Brookline (Frank Chouteau Brown, 1909). The spreading U shape focuses the view on the multicolored tiles of the brick entryway. Although from the street the house looks roughly symmetrical, the rear elevation is quite irregular.

eighteen percent are one-and-one-half stories. Massachusetts architects of English-inspired Arts and Crafts houses used four main devices to influence the viewer's sense of massing: a jettied second floor; a belt course; a pent roof; and a recessed entry or porch. All were methods of breaking up the geometrical shape defined by the smooth surface of the stucco or abetting a sense of horizontality. The jetties were a reference to the medieval English building tradition of cantilevering the second story over the first to gain space for second floor bedrooms, a practice that was replicated by early British settlers in New England and was last extensively used in circa 1925 to 1960 "Garrison Colonials." Usually involving an overhang on the façade, it was surprisingly used in plain stucco more frequently than in "Olde English" half-timbered designs (see Figures 4.5 and 4.6).

The small, single-slope pent roof is set between the first and second floors. Its traditional job is to shelter the entry from inclement weather. But when extended, it can be harnessed to draw the eye to the horizontal line. A good example is 85 Bigelow Road, Newton (see Figure 4.29). This roof was a favorite of Chapman and Frazer who used it in four Arts and Crafts houses in Brookline and this example in Newton.

The belt or string course, a horizontal band generally placed to set off the first from the second story of a building, was usually a feature of masonry architecture but was also used in frame construction. The belt course at the vertically inclined house in Brookline was historically painted in the glittering white of the body (see Figure 2.1) while the contrast-

FIGURE 4.13 34 Century Lane, Milton (Chapman and Frazer, 1912). Here the belt course knits together the different elements of the house, which stretches out horizontally as if to claim the site. The servant wing, usually hidden from view, was placed on the façade, making the house longer.

ing dark color of the belt course of a country retreat in Milton (see Figure 4.13) highlighted the horizontality of the design.

⊰ Roofs ⊱

Roofs do not just cover a house and keep out the weather—they are also shape-givers, image-makers, and lend a comforting sense of shelter. They can refer to another culture, recall a past style, or boldly present a new one. They can complicate or simplify a design. A review of the happy variety of ways Massachusetts architects of the Arts and Crafts used roof shapes reveals their ability to create picturesque designs out of an architectural necessity.

Side Gable Roofs

A gable roof has two pitches, or four in a gambrel, that slope downward from a central ridge and form a gable between them. When the gable is on the side it is called a side or end gable roof. This roof is traditional in New England and was a staple of Georgian and Federal houses. A two-family house in Salem (see Figure 4.14), built in an area decimated by a fire in 1914, is reduced nearly to the essentials but echoes the roof and massing of local Colonial vernacular houses.

Lean-to Roofs

The rear slope of a gable roof can be extended from the ridge to form a lean-to roof. In contrast to early American homeowners who often added a lean-to roofed space to an existing house to gain more room, the houses in this book were designed with them. Employed by architects who admired authentic New England early Colonial houses,

a dwelling in Newton is an example of using a roofline to convey an early American image, although the clipped or jerkin head gables at the roof's end dilute the impression, making the house also look inspired by English vernacular building (see Figures 2.2 and 2.2a).

Front Gable Roofs

Front gable houses, where the main entry is placed in the façade's gable end, were often smaller than those having side gable roofs. A small house in Longmeadow (see Figure 4.15) demonstrates how this limitation can be expanded by a cat-slide extension of the roof.

FIGURE 4.14 76–78 Endicott Street, Salem (probably John Benson, 1916). This modest, two-family house, was erected in fireproof materials although not required by Salem's new fire code, written only after a devastating fire. The design uses a small footprint, simple rectangular shape and Colonial Revival eaves return to enhance the crisp effect of the side gable.

FIGURE 4.15 21 Roseland Terrace, Longmeadow (architect unknown, 1919). The buttress seems intended to reinforce the wall supporting the slope of the catslide roof but was a decorative rather than a structural device.

Hip Roofs

While Massachusetts Arts and Crafts architects more frequently chose to enclose their houses with gable roofs, hip roofs, either in simple or cross-gabled form, account for about one third of the sample. Hip roofs have four shallow or steeply pitched sides that slope down from the ridge. In Massachusetts, they often extended well beyond the house wall, giving the roof a lid-like appearance.

The mid-nineteenth century Gothic Revival style, in rejecting the classical formulas, brought with it the open or raking cornice. Truly open or furnished with a soffit, they continued unabated until the return of the Colonial Revival style brought back to favor the boxed cornice. Swimming against the tide, the roof-wall junction of this hip-roofed Cambridge house (Figure 4.16) is treated with a modified classical boxed cornice relating to its Colonial Revival inflected style. Exemplifying the open cornice in a clipped hipped roof with exposed rafters and purlins is architect Charles Greco's own house (Figure 4.17). (See also Figure 4.4.)

Hip Roof Horizontals

The stunning house of the wealthy and public-minded Nickerson family can represent a small but significant group of hip-roofed examples that stretch out to form long horizontal lines (see Figure 4.18). Mr. Nickerson, the owner, died from the shock of witnessing the fire that demolished the family's large frame vacation house. Soon afterwards, his widow rebuilt an elaborate, cross-hipped mansion in fireproof stucco on the same seaside site. It was unusual to

FIGURE 4.16 43 Reservoir Street, Cambridge (Hartley Dennett, 1909). This is one of the small group of houses in this study poised between the Colonial Revival and Arts and Crafts style. But note the Arts and Crafts motifs of the large trellis on the side elevation and the pergola porch at the rear, both removed in a recent renovation.

FIGURE 4.17 36 Fresh Pond Parkway, Cambridge (Charles R. Greco, 1910). Charles Greco used the ends of the roof's rafters in front and purlins on the side for decorative effect. The Arts and Crafts style in Massachusetts shared this feature with the Craftsman style, with which is it sometimes confused.

FIGURE 4.18 2871 North Main Street, Brewster (Chapman and Frazer, 1919). The repeating lines of the hip-roofed pavilions, each with a bay window, and the buttressed porte cochère further extend the horizontality of the house. The latter feature, closely associated with mansions, kept visitors arriving by carriage or car dry when rainy and provided a grand entry when the weather was fair.

FIGURE 4.19 625 Chestnut Street, Newton (Berry & Davidson, 1913). The cross gable's catslide roof turns a basic house into a dynamic one.

design a grand house in the Arts and Crafts style, but this was a summer home, and therefore somewhat less formal than the norm for very wealthy American vacationers. The interior retains its handcrafted ornate stone fireplaces, mahogany moldings, and lighting fixtures. (Other examples of this group can be seen in Figures 4.13, 4.29, and 4.46.)

Cross Gables

Adding a cross gable perpendicular to a main roof was not only a way of gaining interior space on a restricted suburban lot, it was also a method of adding interest to the design. The cross-gabled roof thus became the most popular form for Massachusetts Arts and Crafts houses. A classic example of a single cross gable, shown in Figure 4.19, is modest in size but bold in execution. Two equal-sized cross gables on a Tudor-themed side gable house make a cozy, semi-enclosed space for the entry (see Figure 4.20). We have seen how the two dramatic, cross gables enliven a hip-roofed house in Newton (see Figure 4.2).

Few Arts and Crafts houses had gambrel roofs, but western Massachusetts architect Karl Scott Putnam used the cross gable skillfully on a gambrel-roofed house (see Figure 4.21). Its octagonal stair tower is a holdover from the Queen Anne style, as was a formal reception room off the hall in addition to the living room, dining room, library, and study.

Catslide Roofs

The catslide descends precipitously from a pitched, hip, or gambrel roof, often to the first-floor level or below. Several

FIGURE 4.20 200 Common Street, Belmont (Allen W. Jackson, 1913–1915). These matching cross gables are emphasized by their jettied upper floor. The half-timbering that separates them is carefully placed to speak, but speak softly.

English Arts and Crafts architects, including Voysey and Parker and Unwin, used the catslide roof to bring a dynamic line to their houses and, when brought below the first-floor level, a sense of shelter (see Figures 1.3, 1.5, and 1.7.) This unexpected line had been a feature of the earlier Queen Anne and Shingle styles, so it was not unknown. However, because Massachusetts architects borrowed from each other as much as from English models, the gesture proved to be something of a signature of the state's style, with about one quarter of the houses in this book displaying it in one form or another.

Part of the catslide's unsettling effect is its asymmetry: one side of the gable being noticeably longer than the other. The resulting diagonal introduces both a sense of instability due to its precipitous pitch and a touch of quirkiness to a design. It was flexible enough for a range of uses. The reader has already seen how strikingly it can be used on a front gable roof house in Longmeadow (see Figure 4.15) and on a dramatic cross gable on a hip roof house (see Figure 4.2). It endows the front entry of a breathtakingly complex house with a bit of pizazz (Figure 4.22), while it shelters within it the entry to a Worcester house (see Figure 4.23), a motif possibly adopted from Parker and Unwin's Letchworth Garden Suburb semidetached houses, or Voysey's 1904 house at

FIGURE 4.21 230 North Main Street, Northampton (Karl Scott Putnam, 1911). Putnam diluted the experience of the gambrel roof by interrupting it with shingled dormers, a cross gable and an octagonal stair tower but brought it into focus again by extending the roof over the screened porch at the side.

Tilehurst. The catslide extends to cover a gated passageway to the rear of a house in Brookline (Figure 4.24), and serves a very different purpose when it is used to help differentiate the units of a two-family house (see Figure 4.25).

FIGURE 4.22 (top left) 32 Everett Avenue, Winchester (possibly Robert Coit, 1908). The abrupt junction of the catslide-roofed entry with the forward-projecting façade is only one of the gestures that gives this house such improbable movement and élan.

FIGURE 4.23 (center) 29 Metcalf Street, Worcester (architect unknown, 1914). The entry is a forerunner of the "storybook" Neo-Tudor houses so popular in the nineteen twenties and thirties.

FIGURE 4.24 (bottom left) 55 Penniman Road, Brookline (Charles D. Maginnis, 1920). The area containing a passageway to the rear was not structurally necessary but offered a good excuse for the dramatic catslide roof, balanced another diagonal on the opposite end and, in extending the house, enhanced the privacy of the backyard.

FIGURE 4.25 (below) 9–11 Hampden Street, Wellesley (Clinton Noble, 1913). Two cross gables define one of the units, the other is almost encompassed by a single gable with a broad catslide.

❧ Dormers ❧

Dormers windows have the task of bringing light and height to low-roofed spaces such as half or attic floors. They are typically set on, or recessed into, the slope of a roof. Beyond this important functional use, they are also harnessed to express a house's stylistic message. We are concerned here with only one somewhat unusual type: the wall dormer that extended through the cornice or eaves in the same plane of the house. Like the catslide roof, Massachusetts architects adapted English Arts and Crafts gestures and made them their own (see Figure 1.8). The appearance of these thrust-

ing dormers in a little dwelling by Putnam and Cox (see Figure 4.26) provides a virtual as well as a metaphorical lift. The spirit of the house was described in *The House Beautiful* in 1920 by Mary Cunningham, a teacher at the nations' first school of architecture and landscape design to admit women, as "intimate, personal, beautiful."[31] A few years later the firm used the same feature with brilliance at a house nearby (see Figure 4.38).

❧ Eaves and Roof ❧

The eaves, the part of the roof that projects from the wall, is an important element in defining the character of a house. Massachusetts homeowners must have believed that nothing says Olde England better than thatching. Although thatch may be made from wheat straw or reeds, no skilled thatchers could be had in Massachusetts: cedar shingle, asphalt, or slate had to substitute for the softer material.

Discussing the use of shingle to imitate thatch, a Ruskinian error, Allen Jackson was skeptical but ambivalent. He considered it not only a "breach of architectural ethics" but also "hard to keep the tongue out of one's cheek." On the other hand, he also thought the result "charming" and a "laudable endeavor to soften the prevailing hardness of outline."[32] And for his own house, James C. Hopkins of Kilham & Hopkins, sought to "give the appearance of an old English home . . . the shingles were rounded over, softening

FIGURE 4.26 41 Crafts Road, Brookline (Putnam & Cox, 1906). The spirit of the house was praised in *The House Beautiful* in 1920 by Mary Cunningham. The sloping roofs over the dormer windows emphasize their upward-thrusting motion, while the French doors and original trellis surrounding the front door anchor the house to the site. The house has since lost the flower boxes she found such an appealing addition.

FIGURE 4.27 105 Rockwood Street, Brookline (J. Lovell Little Jr., 1907). The architect seems to have tried to bestow on this new building the softness of old houses by creating gently rolled eaves.

FIGURE 4.28. 282 Buckminster Road, Brookline (Chapman and Frazer, 1912). Here the angled thatch only faintly recalls the picturesqueness of the authentic vernacular.

the usual hard ridge line."[33] Although critics feared that artificial thatch would flood the market, in fact it never became popular enough to stoke their anxiety for long. The gesture became possible due to two roofing techniques developed in response to the popularity of the Arts and Crafts style.

Rolled Eaves

The first method, used for eaves in a straight line, was to inflate or visually thicken the roof's edge to resemble the bulky look of thatch. The bulging termination of the eaves might be modest or curve inward upon itself. The author of a book on then-modern American country houses, J. Lovell Little Jr. used a house in Brookline to illustrate the gently rolled eaves (Figure 4.27). He opined that the recently developed shingling method here "the curving of the shingle roof is as helpful a one as has yet been found. . . . [it] has not been carried far and yet has immensely aided in relieving the stiffness of the design"[34]. [Another more pronounced example is located at 30 Maplewood Terrace in Springfield (see Figure 4.3).

A beautifully maintained and eye-catching example of the rolled roof is found at the servant's double house in Easton (see Figure 5.3). Although constructed for workingmen—a gardener and a chauffeur—the owner must have paid a good deal to achieve the desired picturesque effect for the passerby.

False Thatch

The second method of achieving a thatched appearance, bending the eaves in angled or curving lines over the upper windows in a dormer-like line, can be termed false thatch. No doubt it was easier to lay eaves in an angled rather than a curving pattern as there are twice as many of the former than the latter. Representative of the angled type is a house

75

FIGURE 4.29 85 Bigelow Road, Newton (Chapman and Frazer, 1913). It is evident that the deeply curving lines of the eaves lends much of the sought-after charm of the original models.

by Chapman and Frazer (Figure 4.28). The rolling curves of the eaves of an engaging house by the same firm were executed in slate (see Figure 4.29).

❧ Entries ❧

The entries of English-influenced Arts and Crafts houses share the diversity of the group's designs and relative freedom from classical architecture's focus on the door surround: their variety is delightful but difficult to categorize. They can be recessed into the body of the house; topped by a hood; embellished with a portico; trimmed with half-timbering; sheltered by a pent roof; placed under a porch; or simply let into the front or side wall. Only the most distinctively American of the English-inspired Arts and Crafts adaptations are discussed below.

Columned and Pillared Entries

Not surprisingly, given their long use in American houses and New England's snowy winters and rainy springs, Arts and Crafts architects widely employed little columned porticos to shelter the entry. They include variations of the classical (see Figure 4.16), Craftsman (Figure 4.17), and faintly Tudor styles (Figure 4.30).

In a less formal vein, Massachusetts architects developed a short, fat, stucco-covered column that seemed to be vernacular and its peasant sturdiness appropriate for an Arts and Crafts house. A little house in Springfield

FIGURE 4.30 150 Monadnock Road, Newton (architect unknown, 1919). The small, rather insubstantial entry is given the whole task of defining a Tudor inflection for this Arts and Crafts house.

(see Figure 4.31) reads as big due to its bold catslide roof supported by squat columns and hefty, deeply curved braces. Since the columns are in proportion to the massing, they do not look awkward but have an attractive humor. (See also Figure 4.19).

Recessed Entry

Among the many types, the recessed entry was a favorite of Arts and Crafts architects. Perhaps because these houses looked like solid masonry, though they were usually wood frame with stucco coating, their smooth solidity seemed made for an entry carved out of the mass and drawing the visitor in. To emphasize the void rather than the surface, the recessed entry was often left unadorned, as in Figure 4.32.

FIGURE 4.32 17 Everett Avenue, Winchester (Robert Coit, 1907). The deep recess of the entry, with its setback door and flanking half-sidelights, subtly helps balance the asymmetry of the house, allowing it to look at once formal and informal..

Recessed and Columned Entry

Several architects applied the ancient formula, in Classical architecture known as in antis, of using two columns to support the lintel of a recessed space. Surprisingly, eight houses employed this strategy for an entry or secondary porch (see Figures 4.18 and 4.45).

Battered Entries

Although English Arts and Crafts architects used buttressing as expressive and structural elements in their houses, they infrequently employed it as part of the entry. However, there are ten examples in Massachusetts associating a battered wall—one sloped like a buttress—with an entry. Perhaps Bay State residents recognized battering as a dramatic, historicizing trope of the Arts and Crafts movement.

FIGURE 4.31 36 Maplewood Terrace, Springfield (1912). Pulling back the columns from the edge of the low porch heightens the experience of this deeply sheltered entry.

Variations include battering an entrance porch (Figure 4.4), or porch columns as in a house by Robert Coit in Winchester (Figure 4.53).

❧ Windows ❧

Windows were conventionally said to be the eyes of a house and described as its most expressive feature. While an overstatement, they have much to do with defining the character of a building.

Grouped or Banked

Certainly, not every English Arts and Crafts house accessible to Massachusetts architects in book or magazine form was lit by windows grouped in pairs, triplets, or larger multiples, but many featured this gesture. J. Lovell Little Jr., in a 1910 *House and Garden* article on "Modern English Plaster Houses for America," spread this design concept when he illustrated it with a house by English architect Edwin Lutyens that had a successful grouping of small windows (see Figures 1.1 through 1.8). The adjective "small" is key here: one critic, in comparing American and English windows stated that Voysey's windows were "reduced . . . to a size which no American owner would permit, largely because of our hotter summers."[35] This is probably only a part of the explanation, the English thought smaller windows were more picturesque and lent an air of mystery, while Americans had little desire for mystery.

A 1909 comment on the Massachusetts house pictured in Figure 4.32 cites the banked fenestration as critical to its attractiveness—"An unusually pretty suburban house is that designed by Mr. Robert Coit of Boston, Massachusetts. . . . Here again the effective grouping of the windows relieves the broad exterior surfaces."[36] Because banked windows introduced a horizontal line that broke from the generally vertical fenestration of the previous Queen Anne style, the gesture was common to all the Arts and Crafts variations in the United States—Craftsman, Greene and Greene, Northern California, Prairie, and the New York, New Jersey, and Pennsylvania types. Both double-hung and casement windows could be effectively grouped, often in a single house (see Figure 4.25).

Casements

Also adopted from the English Arts and Crafts vocabulary was the side-hinged casement window, used in England since the seventeenth century and brought to Massachusetts by the first settlers who installed them as soon as they were able. However, beginning in the eighteenth and gathering force in the invention-rich nineteenth century, casements were largely replaced by movable sash windows in England and almost entirely so in America. Yet, English Arts and Crafts architects, yearning for simpler, bucolic, and more traditional times, sought the revival of the casement as an emblem of the nostalgia-tinged pre-industrial past. A popular New York architect in 1904 argued that in stucco houses "plain wall surfaces and grouped windows are characteristic of the best work. Casement windows seem particularly appropriate and good for houses of this sort. The prejudice against them in this country is rapidly disappearing, now that our architects are learning how to construct them properly."[37] A year earlier, Frank Chouteau Brown had, with more hope than realism, called the double-hung window "old fashioned." Allen Jackson believed casements were one of the elements that added to the "hominess of the English house"[38] and argued for their use in this country.

It would be, however, an uphill battle to convince Americans to give up their convenient and weather-tight

CASEMENT WINDOWS
are the most convenient things in the world when controlled by the
Sperry Casement Lock and Adjuster
This device, opens, closes and locks the window, holding same rigidly in any desired position, all without disturbing inside screen or draperies. Thousands in use giving perfect satisfaction. Write us for full information.
OSCAR C. RIXSON CO. 111 W. HARRISON ST. CHICAGO

FIGURE 4.33 An advertisement for casement window hardware in The House Beautiful (November 1908). A remarkable number of the original casements remain: evidence their homeowners are willing to maintain rather than replace them.

double-hung windows for an antique gesture. I imagine that Arts and Crafts architects made a valiant attempt. Architect Thomas Mott Shaw was particularly fond of grouping multiple windows for an arresting effect. At a house for his probably compliant sister in Concord (Figure 4.34; façade illustrated in Figure 4.11), he arranged the rear elevation as a display of casements and French doors matching the windows, flooding the rooms with light.[39] Not the least of the problems with casements was that until 1906, no mechanism had been developed to open them without disturbing screens and storm windows or make possible the convenient cleaning of their exteriors. But even with an invention that solved all three of these problems, the casement never became America's window. (See Figure 4.33)

Double-hung windows

More than a decade after the invention of the mechanisms that rendered the casement more conveniently operable,

FIGURE 4.34 345 Garfield Road, Concord (Thomas Mott Shaw, 1909). Shaw gave the garden elevation at the rear of the house a high perch, with a terrace overlooking a dramatic rock outcropping. Since privacy was not an issue on this generous estate, he could expose the entire elevation to light and view.

Ekin Wallick stated that they had "not become popular yet in this country. As a matter of fact, our double hung sashes are more practical and by using the small paned windows, we get very much the same effect."[40] He assured his readers that proportionally short and broad windows would yield what he believed owners of an Arts and Crafts house were aiming for, "a very quaint appearance to the exterior."[41] Although large panes of glass had been available since the mid-nineteenth century, and became more popular after the invention of machine-manufactured glass at the end of the century, Arts and Crafts, Colonial Revival, and Craftsman styles called for multiple lights to reference historic architecture. A wide majority of the houses in this study have at least six or eight lights in the upper sash and most have multiple lights in both upper and lower double-hung windows.

Bays and Bows and Oriel Windows

Rectangular or polygonal bays, rounded bows, and un-supported oriel windows gained popularity in the United States in the 1840s and 1850s with the Gothic Revival and Italianate styles and continued even more so thereafter. By the burgeoning of the Arts and Crafts in Massachusetts these windowed protrusions from the wall had been common for a half-century as prized vehicles for bringing additional light, space, expanded views, and interest into a room. English Arts and Crafts architects used them liberally and Massachusetts architects who followed saw no rea-

FIGURE 4.35 200 Common Street, Belmont (Allen W. Jackson, 1913–1915). These wide, leaded glass two-story bay windows suggest an almost palpable connection between the well-lit interior and secluded garden to the rear.

son not to do the same. Several houses in this study, such as the house illustrated in Figure 4.9, display more than one type. About one half are furnished with at least one such window, with bays well in the lead.

The shallow, copper-roofed rectangular bay of a house in Winchester (see Figure 4.32) balances the façade. The architect tiled the sill in the dining room's bay window

FIGURE 4.36. 3 Clement Circle, Cambridge (Charles K. Cummings, 1903). The generous, casement-filled oriel opens up the façade and provides a wider view than would a standard window.

FIGURE 4.37. 173 Bellevue Road, Watertown (Frank Chouteau Brown, 1912). The little oriel on brackets on the second story with its high peaked roof looks almost like a miniature house and is essential to the originality of the composition.

for a sunny ledge to please a plant-loving client. The hexagonal-shaped, two-story bay window was common in England but unusual in Massachusetts (see Figure 1.4). Architect Allen W. Jackson used a two-story bay to make the garden elevation of a house in Belmont (Figure 4.35) almost as important as its façade. At a house in Newton whose side-facing façade is hard to see from the street, a generous, leaded bow window gives the passerby a pleasant focus (see Figures 2.2a and 2.2b).

Oriels, because they are suspended and not supported by the ground, can be used on the upper floors as well as the first, and were so popular that almost 20 percent of the houses in this study had one. The large oriel of a Cambridge house appears heavy in this early photograph (Figure 4.36), but landscaping and foundation plantings have softened its lines to make it much more attractive. Second floor oriels

can be more fanciful, as seen in Frank Chouteau Brown's masterful composition of materials and steeply roofed oriel in Figure 4.37. A two-story oriel, likely a stair window, is a focal point of an appealing house by Putnam & Cox in Brookline (see Figure 4.38).

FIGURE 4.38. 35 Spooner Road, Brookline (Putnam and Cox, 1911). This oriel, just to the left of the doorway and probably lighting the staircase, is unusual because it is so tall and makes the one and one-half story house appear larger than it is. The wide, through-the-eaves dormer continues that upward movement.

Like their choice of old-fashioned casements instead of double-hung windows, English Arts and Crafts architects tried to eschew large single panes of glass for many small ones, leaded together by craftsmen. Indeed, prominent English Arts and Crafts architect M. H. Baillie Scott sturdily maintained he could "recall no example of building where the windows are formed of large sheets of glass which have survived their disastrous effect."[42] Barry Parker urged the public to "Think of the beauty of leaded glass compared to

the lifeless hard mechanical perfection of polished plate. The beauty has nothing to do with its old-fashioned look, with romantic associations or quaintness of effect."[43] Rather, he thought, it was due to the quality of light of leaded glazing, the endless "charm of the play of light and shade on different panes,"[44] each of which caught the light differently. The Massachusetts architectural critic, Mary H. Northend, was, however, attracted to exactly the easy romanticism Parker rejected when she said of a Newton house (see Figures 2.2a and 2.2b), "The small lights of glass, with which the quaint grouped windows are fitted, strengthens the effect of the old English type of cottage. . . ."[45]

In defense of architects specifying leaded casements, it must be admitted that, from the outside, the many small panes present an orderly, human-scaled composition, understandable as a collection of units that readily fit in one's hand, while from the inside, the experience of looking out is particularly pleasant, especially if the scene on the other side is attractive and does not require a long view (see Figure 4.39). About one-fifth of the houses in this study have at least one operable leaded glass window or one fixed light such as sidelights. Because lead-glazed windows were more expensive than plate, they were often used in the important downstairs public rooms while double-hung windows, sometimes having multiple but not leaded panes in the upper sash, were provided for the rooms upstairs (see Figure 4.56). Elegant and delicate sidelights frame the door of a Cambridge house in Figure 4.40. (For the exterior of this house, see Figure 4.9.)

FIGURE 4.39. 11–15 Elmwood Avenue, Cambridge (Allen W. Jackson, 1908). The lead cams or fasteners and the many panes, while barely limiting the casement's transparency, can increase the sense of privacy as this window looks out on the street.

FIGURE 4.40 117 Lake View Avenue, Cambridge (C. H. Bartlett, 1910). Few English-inspired Arts and Crafts houses in Massachusetts employed leaded glass in the sidelights of the main entry. An exception is this unusual pattern in a house full of interior handcrafted detail.

Stained Glass

Given the proclivity for architects and builders alike to specify stained glass, often from catalogues, in the houses built in the decades proceeding the English-inspired Arts and Crafts style in Massachusetts, it was surprising to find so little in the houses discussed here. In 1907, Massachusetts architect, artist, and craftsman Addison LeBoutillier inveighed against the poor design of then-available com-

mercial stained glass, strangely without discussing the excellent Prairie School work. "No wonder . . . that people of refinement are prejudiced against stained glass in their homes. They could not live with it. It is bad enough to spend an hour or two in its garish light once a week at church."[46]

The single use of painted-on glass occurs in perhaps the most expensive and lavishly decorated house among them, the Nickerson mansion in Brewster, shown in Figure 4.41. (See also Figure 4.18.) Surrounded by hexagonal bull-seye glass recalling an "Olde English" technique, the light-hearted glass roundels were intended for the inhabitants and their guests, not for the public. Their gaily painted and evocative images suggest comforting nursery rhymes in clear colors and stereotypical figures.

FIGURE 4.41 2871 North Main Street, Brewster (Chapman and Frazer, 1919). Arts and Crafts architects of the Northwest, Southern California, Prairie and Craftsman styles used stained glass extensively, but those working in Massachusetts did not, perhaps because of the scarcity of suitable designs.

⊰ Porches ⊱

Living Porches

Architectural commentators maintained that while the English invariably preferred a rear terrace in their garden, Americans favored covered porches, called in the first decades of the twentieth century a living-porch or piazza. The porch, a nearly standard feature of Massachusetts domestic architecture since the late nineteenth century, was used in the twentieth as one of several strategies, such as pergolas, trellises, and flowerboxes to link the house and its occupants to its landscape or the street. In contrast to the Queen Anne and Shingle Styles' wraparound or wide front porches, Arts and Crafts porches in Massachusetts tended to be set discretely on side or back elevations or indented into the body of the house. Set on a narrow lot, the now glazed but originally screened porch on a Brookline house (Figure 4.42) is located at the side of the façade. The unusual, sketched-in roofed space of architect Charles Greco's own home blurred the line between porch and terrace (see Figure 4.43).

FIGURE 4.42 37 Salisbury Road, Brookline (Putnam & Alden, 1911–1912). The contemporary search for more interior space has meant the filling of many originally open or screened porches.

FIGURE 4.43 36 Fresh Pond Parkway, Cambridge (Charles Greco, 1910). Greco built in the panoply of early twentieth century styles, but for his family's use he chose the English-inspired Arts and Crafts, flavored with a sophisticated Craftsman entry and porch.

The sleeping porch, which gained popularity in houses of all styles in the first decade of the twentieth century, was a new concept. It was the product of a combined health fad and an increasingly affordable mechanical invention. The first was a reaction to the invalidated nineteenth-century notion that "night air" was full of dangerous miasmas, to be kept at bay by tight bedroom windows and nightcaps. With the general acceptance of the theory that, instead, it was bacteria and viruses that spread disease, fresh air was thought to be restorative as well as a natural form of air conditioning. The sleeping porch became a physical expression of this notion and a cutting-edge feature of home design. The invention that made it possible was inexpensive, permanent, or temporary wire screening that barred insects and critters from annoying slumbering fresh air advocates. An ad in a popular shelter magazine traded on parents' dread of typhoid to increase sales by prominently featuring the trusted family doctor and a nurse hovering near the bed of a sick child. The doctor's solution was to "prescribe" Pearl Wire Cloth screening (see Figure 4.44).[47]

A 1914 article in *House and Garden* linked the growing number of Americans leaving the farms to work indoors in factories and offices to the necessity of having a sleeping porch. Sleeping outdoors was not only believed to promote good health but was positively "efficacious in the treatment of disease. Those who during the day are de-

FIGURE 4.44 An advertisement for screens in *The House Beautiful* (June 1919). Because health fads are generally short-lived enthusiasms, unsupported by scientific fact, the fad for sleeping porches as essential for health did not last long. But the sleeping porches themselves remained long past their heyday.

FIGURE 4.45 33 Circuit Road, Brookline (J. Lovell Little Jr., 1907). The house appeared in an article by the architect in The Architectural Review in 1907, and in the same journal in 1909 with a photograph prominently featuring the recently added living and sleeping porches. The 1909 caption stated the house was "simple in form and detail and with all unnecessary 'architecture' eliminated. . . ." probably meaning the absence of historicizing ornamentation.

FIGURE 4.46 16 Berkeley Street, Cambridge (Harley Dennett, 1905). This sleeping porch overlooks a quiet garden to the rear.

prived of the necessary allowance of fresh air must obtain it during the night."[48] According to an almost certainly exaggerated statement, by 1921 sleeping porches had become so popular that "The problem of the sleeping porch is one which has to be met by almost every architect in almost every house."[49] These semi-outdoor rooms were optimally located adjacent to the second floor bedrooms for easy use, but suspending an open porch aloft could be unsightly if not carefully designed.

FIGURE 4.47 23 Newmarch Street, Ipswich (architect unknown, ca. 1905). This sleeping porch and its twin on the opposite elevation are part of the decorative design. They serve two of the three bedrooms in the house.

An excellent example is the airy Brookline sleeping porch located over a screened porch off the living room. The two were added by J. Lovell Little Jr., who had conscientiously designed the house a few years earlier with room for this expansion (see Figure 4.45). A sleeping porch could also be recessed into the house, as in the upper left-hand

corner of a Cambridge Arts and Crafts house with Colonial Revival overtones (Figure 4.46). For a house sited on a hill in Ipswich whose garden elevation looks down on the Ipswich River, an unknown architect placed two generously scaled sleeping porches to ensure sweeping views of the dramatic landscape. (See Figure 4.47.)

⌁ Surface Treatments ⌁

Although simplicity was assumed to be the watchword of the Arts and Crafts movement, it has always been understood in a relative sense: one generation's simple is another's fussy. In fact, especially in comparison with the Queen Anne house which prized an exterior complicated by shape and surface, most Arts and Crafts houses of Massachusetts display an uncluttered appearance. But local architects would not renounce all exterior attempts to enhance the surface of their houses.

Half-Timbering

Half-timbering describes the use of dark-stained, heavy timbers as structural members exposed on a building's exterior, with the spaces between filled with brick or, more commonly, smooth contrasting plaster. A feature of English domestic architecture dating from the end of the Middle Ages, it became increasingly important during the Tudor period. With the blossoming in England of the Gothic-influenced Tudor Revival style in the 1880s, revivalist and Arts and Crafts architects took up the motif with a decorative rather than a structural purpose. The English Arts and Crafts architect Edwin Lutyens was fond of incorporating short runs of the technique, as seen at one of his masterpieces, Munstead Wood (see Figure 1.5).

Americans were of two minds about this building technique, as seen in conflicting statements by an architect practicing in New York. "Half-timber work as constructed nowadays is never anything but a sham—the imitation of an abandoned method of construction—and for that reason, despite its picturesqueness, it is not recommended. When architecture ceases to be logical, it ceases to be good." But he reversed himself when he continued "However, when the half-timber work is confined to an occasional gable . . . no serious objection can be raised against it, for the effect is charming. . . ."[50] The architect and critic Frank Chouteau Brown, however, thought the use of this "exotic style" in contemporary work "purely sentimental," of "dubious morality," and essentially unfit for American building.[51]

Architect Allen W. Jackson, who was deeply attracted to half-timbering, wrote a book entitled *The Half-Timber House* to "protest against the stereotyped use of certain historical styles for contemporary use, and plea for a greater freshness and vitality than is often found in the work of today."[52] While he agreed that timber work was dangerous and should be used as sparingly as a jewel, he was sure that it gave a "picturesque individuality"[53] to a house. In construction, Jackson advocated repurposing old, distressed timbers from other structures to soften a house's appearance and create

FIGURE 4.48 227 Mason Terrace, Brookline (Harry M. Ramsey, 1915). Harry Ramsey, an extremely prolific architect, packed an array of Arts and Crafts gestures into a small space, including the catslide roof extending to an arched entry in the wingwall. The Tudoresque bargeboards and restrained half-timbering lend the house a romantic, medieval air.

FIGURE 4.49 14 Huntington Road, Newton (Chapman and Frazer, 1919). Here the exterior chimney disrupts the symmetry of this dramatic elevation. Protruding rooms containing a billiard room and a glazed piazza, now altered, and flank a central recessed entrance and terrace. A still existing pergola at the rear afforded another defined garden area.

the necessary "charm" and did so himself, but was significantly less enthusiastic about embedding thin planks in the stucco. If thin pieces of wood were decoratively applied to the surface, Jackson was adamant that the planks must have no hard edges, be unevenly finished with a hand adze or retain their coarse mill surfaces, and, to achieve a rough, masculine appearance, remain unpainted and treated with a preservative.

Jackson used his own house in Cambridge to illustrate the restrained use of half-timber work in an elevation that expresses its plan (see Figure 4.5). Another of his designs placed closely spaced half-timbering to emphasize the entrance at the center (see Figure 4.20). A house in Brookline (Figure 4.48) uses even less timbering than at Jackson's own house to imply a Tudor connection.

Exterior Chimneys

English Arts and Crafts architects, particularly Lutyens, often made the massive exterior chimney a significant element of their design. Massachusetts architects influenced by them tended to include these chimneys as objects of punctuation and pleasant elements, but they were generally neither as imposing nor as elaborately detailed as the models from which they were drawn. An exterior chimney acts like an exclamation point in the U-shaped composition of

FIGURE 4.50 61 Stone Road, Belmont (architect unknown, 1915). Exterior chimneys are vulnerable to the snow and rain that can create cracks in the surface of the stucco. Here the red tiles of the successively smaller chimney shoulders help to prevent water damage and provide a lively detail.

FIGURE 4.51 20 Sylvan Avenue, Newton (architect unknown, 1911). This unique arrangement of leaded-glass windows butting up against an out-sized chimney gives a focal point to the street elevation and probably provides a snug window seat for contemplation on the interior.

an elevation made active with three wall dormers (see Figure 4.49). The red-tiled and stepped gradations of the chimney shoulders of a house in Belmont (Figure 4.50) play a noteworthy role in enhancing its modest design. Perhaps because the façade of a suburban house faces a nearby side lot line and so is difficult to see, visitors approaching the house are greeted instead with a bold, original feature on the street-side elevation: an exterior chimney flanked on the second floor by bay windows and embellished with a trellis for eye-catching effect (see Figure 4.51). Another method of dealing with an exterior chimney is to erect it patterned in contrasting brick colors instead of plaster (Figure 4.52).

FIGURE 4.52 20 Common Street, Belmont (Allen W. Jackson, 1912). Two-color brickwork in diapered patterns goes back to Tudor practice, as the architectural scholar Jackson would have known. Here the pattern is achieved with red stretchers and brown headers rather than a common, more uniform bonding technique.

FIGURE 4.53 3 Sheffield Road West, Winchester (Robert Coit, 1914). Coit built over fifty houses in Winchester, his hometown. Strangely, for a house built on speculation for a local developer, this is one of his more unusual exteriors, although the interior plan was conventional for its period.

Exterior Tiles

Although stucco's monotone texture and color were prized for their large, simple surfaces on which to strategically locate openings, English and American architects occasionally placed colorful tiles on them. An outstanding example is the house Robert Coit designed in Newton with tiles deployed to balance the two major masses (see Figure 4.2). At another vigorous house by Coit in Winchester, the architect used the same simple diamond shapes laid out in a diamond pattern, even on the external chimney. Seen in an early photograph, the tiles had more impact when they were painted in a contrasting color and before the current balcony and rail were placed atop the unusually tall battered columns.[54] (Figure 4.53.) One of the most imaginative uses of tile is seen in a house of the owner of a tile importing business (see Figure 4.12). Architect Frank Chouteau Brown used both the exterior and interior to illustrate the versatility and beauty of the material (see Figure 4.54).

FIGURE 4.54 3219 Buckminster Road, Brookline (Frank Chouteau Brown, 1909). This is the only example of the insertion of tiny tiles on a brick or stucco exterior in this study. It is lovingly accomplished.

FIGURE 4.55 88 Farlow Road, Newton (Chapman and Frazer, 1917). The window box focuses attention on the deep hood over the entry, which replicates the curve of the false thatch in the eaves.

Lattice

In the first decades of the twentieth century, many believed that an application of lattice or trellising was a winning recipe for applying the necessary romantic quality to the English-inspired Arts and Crafts house. At least one commentator thought they represented contemporary practice, although perhaps harking back to the past, "The greatly increasing use of lattice-work, both as a purely decorative feature, and as a trellis for vines, is . . . characteristic of the modern work."[55] In addition, vines growing on trellises were "an invaluable link between the structure and grounds, conveying a sense of fitness of the house to the site."[56] It is probable that many more examples of lattices and trellises existed on the examples in this book but were not replaced when they deteriorated or were damaged in the course of

house painting. For example, at the house J. Lovell Little Jr. designed at 33 Circuit Avenue, Brookline, (see Figure 4.45) both the lattices that originally surrounded the two groups of first-floor windows and the window boxes of the second floor have recently disappeared.

In Frank Chouteau Brown's house in Watertown, the architect called on a variety of materials: a shingled second floor above a stucco first floor whose porch columns are of fieldstone and wood, while he surrounded the first-floor windows of a street-facing wall with a dense scrim of trellis and greenery. It makes for a composition of movement, whimsy and surprising harmony (see Figure 4.37).

Window Boxes

Window boxes may be the most impermanent of all the surface elaborations due to their exposure to the weather and the vagaries of the residents' interest. Although the first century Romans used them, spreading the custom to Europe and England and eventually to Colonial New England, they do not seem to have been popular in nineteenth-century Massachusetts. But at the opening of the twentieth century they might have been received as a fresh way to increase the cheerful coziness of a house. At least eighteen of the houses in this study had one or more. The single window box on a house in Newton (Figure 4.55), which has plenty of pleasures in the false thatch, eyebrow window, and multiple porches, adds one more with an overflowing window box.

FIGURE 4.56 26 Beech Road, Brookline (Hartwell, Richardson and Driver, 1907). The delicacy and extent of this carving is remarkable. The unusual full-length, railed terrace functions to set off the house from the wide mall planted with rows of beech trees it faces.

Carved Decoration

Only three houses in this study have significant exterior carving but one calls for illustration. The Brookline house by Hartwell, Richardson and Driver employs lacy and sculptural carving finely crafted in wood: it adorns the pedimented entry portico and brackets supporting the jettied gable blocks. The carved owls perched on the terrace rail near the entrance may have been intended to repel crows, but they also entertain human visitors. (See Figures 4.56 and 4.56a.)

⁘ Extensions into the Landscape ⁘

Pergolas

The pergola, a garden walk usually formed by two rows of posts loosely roofed to support vines, was an ancient idea. Garden designers for English Arts and Crafts houses enthusiastically endorsed them for their cozy shade and ability to lead the eye into the landscape and craftsman Gustav Stickley opined that a pergola in the garden "is the spirit of the outdoor environment held in one place to welcome you."[57] Although *The House Beautiful* magazine told its readers in 1919 they could be purchased from manufacturers and their rectangular lines harmonized well with "cement"

FIGURE 4.56A . 26 Beech Road, Brookline (Hartwell, Richardson and Driver, 1907). Seen closer, the vivid human and lion faces, stylized leaves and flowers engage the viewers' attention.

FIGURE 4.57 61 Spooner Road, Brookline (Chapman and Frazer, 1914). Arts and Crafts clients must have believed with craftsman Gustav Stickley that Americans needed an outdoor life. He wrote that a pergola in the garden "is the spirit of the outdoor environment held in one place to welcome you."

houses, local Arts and Crafts architects often specified them as squat stucco columns, probably built on the spot.[58] An example is found on a modest lot in Brookline (Fiugre 4.57) where the pergola becomes an extension of the porch rather than a path through the garden.

Wing walls

Another method of extending the house to the landscape, while also screening the back yard, was to attach a wing wall to a house so that it lengthened the façade. English architects used walls in abundance to define changes in

ground levels and to enclose garden and courtyard spaces, but they seldom used wing walls. Massachusetts architects, perhaps because they were dealing with smaller lots, often highlighted them as shown in this exuberant example (Figure 4.58) in Wellesley. (See also Figure 4.48.)

In sum, we can say that Massachusetts architects tended to pick and choose from among those Arts and Crafts gestures developed by English architects in a process of selection rather than wholesale copying. In a parallel manner, Massachusetts Arts and Crafts architects borrowed ideas from each other even more than they did from the

FIGURE 4.58 .12 Leighton Road, Wellesley (Clinton Noble, 1915). The extended, curving wing wall, a significant part of the design, is another instance of Massachusetts architects borrowing gestures from each other.

English. Perhaps this is how all styles are created, a zeitgeist emerges that seems obvious to the makers of society until it ceases to express the tempo and needs of the time. And then it is a thing of the past. However, a few lingering motifs in modified form lived on in the Neo-Tudor style of the 1920s and 1930s storybook houses. Half-timbering employed as trim remained an identifying element while the even more exaggerated catslide roofs of the 1920s and 1930s capped small but high gabled entries.

J. Lovell Little Jr., one of the most perceptive of Massachusetts architectural critics, held that English plaster houses were both economically reasonable and practical to build. Of their aesthetic values, the most significant was simplicity, which should be the "keynote of the design of the average American suburban or country house."[59] He believed that these homegrown interpretations of the English Arts and Crafts movement, dependent as they were on proportions, the spacing and arrangement of window openings in relation to walls and the logical expression of interior arrangements on the exterior, would result in an authentic American style. Not all the houses in this book live up to his lofty ideals, but many make the attempt and most succeed. This American style lasted for domestic architecture in Massachusetts from just after the turn of the twentieth century until nearly a quarter of a century later. In a period of rapid change, it was eventually effaced by a patriotic devotion to the Neo-Georgian and Neo-Federal styles that were increasingly stiffly modeled on the homes and buildings of the safest of American icons, the colonial settlers and the founding fathers.

1   Builders found granite along the coasts north and south of Boston and a few deposits inland in the seventeenth century, but improvements in quarrying and working the stone sufficient for using it for ordinary houses did not occur until the early nineteenth century. Even then, unless near the quarry site, housebuilding in granite was prohibitively expensive, although the stone was often used for foundations.

2   M. K. Zimerman, "Pittsburg, PA," *The Brick and Clay Record* 44, no. 7 (Chicago: Kensfield-Leach Co., April 7, 1914), 843. The author used the phrase in quotes when stating that the "'stucco craze' would have been longer lived" had it not been for the new ideas in brick manufacture and laying. A year earlier in the same publication, he stated that "the stucco craze seems to have run its course."

3   Building Trades Employees' Association, "Stucco Used Extensively Centuries Ago," *Bulletin* 10, no. 6 (New York: June 1909), 86.

4   "Points in Favor of the Stucco House," *Keith's Magazine: On Homebuilding* XXX, no. 5 (Minneapolis: November 1913), 335.

5   Ibid., 335.

6   *Structural Conservation*, June–July 1916.

7   F. B. Brown, "Exterior Plaster Construction I," *The Architectural Review* 14, no. 1 (January 1907), 1.

8   David I. Barnes, "The Value of Stucco," *The House Beautiful* (June 1919), 349.

9   Mary H. Northland, "A House at Newton, Massachusetts," *American Homes and Gardens* (December 1912), 428.

10 Ibid.

11 Allen W. Jackson, "Homes that Architects Have Built for Themselves," 323.

12 Ekin Wallick, *The Small House for a Moderate Income*, 53.

13 William L. Price, "Model Houses: A $3500 To $4000 Suburban House," in William L. Price and William L Johnson, *Home Building and Furnishing* (New York: Doubleday, Page and Co., 1903), 4.

14 James C. Hopkins, "An Architect's Solution of His Own House and Garden Problems," *The American Architect* XCIX, no. 1842 (April 1911), 139.

15 Allen W. Jackson, *The Half-Timber House* (New York: McBride, Nast and Co., 1912), 58.

16 The first bay on the right, now filled, was originally a small porch with arched openings on the front and side elevations.

17 J. Lovell Little Jr., "House at Chestnut Hill, Massachusetts," *The Architectural Review* XIV, no. 3 (March 1907), 39.

18 Frank Chouteau Brown, "Modern English Suburban Houses II," *The Brickbuilder* 16, no. 1 (January 1907), 8.

19 J. Lovell Little Jr., "A $5,000 House for a Family of Four," *Indoors and Out* 1, no. 4 (January 1906), 191.

20 Ibid.

21 Frank Chouteau Brown, "Suburban Homes," *Good Housekeeping* 38, no. 4 (October 1903), 12.

22 Ibid.

23 Allen W. Jackson, *The Half-Timber House*, 41.

24 J. Lovell Little Jr., "Modern English Plaster Houses for America: Why the Type of Plaster House That Is Being Built in England To-Day Comes Nearest to Fulfilling the American Requirements" *House and Garden* 17, no. 3 (March 1910), 97.

25 Ibid.

26 Oswald Hering, *Concrete and Stucco Houses: The Use of Plastic Materials in the Building of Country and Suburban Houses* (New York: The Country House Library, McBride, Nast & Co., 1912), 113.

27 Lois Lily Howe, "Serving Pantries in Small Houses," *The Architectural Review* XIV, no. III (March 1907), 31.

28 Frank Chouteau Brown, "Suburban Houses," *Good Housekeeping* XXXVIII, no. 4 (October 1903), 302.

29 H. W. Frohne, "Recent English Domestic Architecture," *The Architectural Record* 25 (April 4, 1909), 261.

30 This shape was known in English Arts and Crafts work as the butterfly plan, while the space between the wings was called a suntrap.

31 Cunningham, Mary P. "A Small House Which Revels in Flowers," *The House Beautiful*, November 1920, House Beautiful Publishing Co., XLVIII, V, 387.

32 Allen W. Jackson. *The Half-Timber House*, 27–28.

33 James C. Hopkins, *An Architect's Solution.*, 142.

34 Aymar Embury II, *One Hundred Country Houses*, 198.

35 Aymar Embury II, *One Hundred Country Houses*, 164.

36 Benjamin A. Howes, "The Use of Concrete in the Building of the Small Country House," *American Homes and Gardens* (April 1909), 165.

37 Claude Bragdon, "Plaster Houses," *The Architectural Review* XI, no. 1 (January 1904), 21.

38 Allen W. Jackson, "Homes that Architects Have Built for Themselves," 295.

39 The first-floor bay on the far right was originally a recessed, columned porch, now filled. For the original see *Current Architecture: Yearbook of the Boston Architectural Club* (Boston: The Boston Architectural Club, 1916), 11.

40 Ekin Wallick, *The Small House for a Moderate Income*, 35.

41 Ibid.

42 M. H. Baillie Scott, *Houses and Gardens* (London: George Newnes Ltd., 1906), 66.

43 Barry Parker, "The Dignity of All True Art," *The Art of Building a Home* (London: Longmans, Green and Co., Mayfield Press, 1901), 32.

44 Ibid.

45 Mary H. Northland, "The Interesting Stucco House," 386.

46 Addison LeBoutiller, "Modern Designs for Domestic Leaded Glass," *The Architectural Review* XIV, no. 2 (December 1907), 233.

47 Pearl Wire Cloth advertisement, *The House Beautiful* (June 1919), 378.

48 Fredrick N. Reed, "The Problem of the Sleeping Porch," *House & Garden* XXV, no. 6 (June 1914), 462.

49 Bragg and Neukirk, "A Novel Sleeping Porch," *House Beautiful* XLIX, no. 11 (February 1921), 121.

50 Claude Bragdon, "Plaster Houses," *The Architectural Review* XI, no. 1 (January 1904), 22.

51 Frank Chouteau Brown, "The Relation Between English and American Domestic Architecture: Modern Work in England," *The Brickbuilder* 15, no. 10 (October 1906), 210. Brown did however illustrate Alan Jackson's book on half-timbering.

52 Allen W. Jackson, *The Half Timber House*, xi.

53 Allen W. Jackson, "The Case for the Half-timber House," *House & Garden* 17, no. 10 (January 1910), 6.

54 Ellen Spencer, "Robert Coit: Houses and Public Buildings in an Age of Suburban Growth," *The Architects of Winchester, Massachusetts*, Inventory #8, (Winchester, MA: Winchester Historical Society, 2007).

55 Aymar Embury II, *One Hundred Country Houses*, 14.

56 Ibid., 15.

57 Gustav Stickley. *More Craftsman Homes*, (NY: The Craftsman Publishing Co., 1912), 178.

58 C. W. Moores, "Rose Trellises for Stucco Walls," *The House Beautiful* (June 1919), 368.

59 J. Lovell Little Jr., "Modern English Plaster Houses," 31.

Chapter Five
ARTS AND CRAFTS HOUSING
FOR SERVANTS, WORKERS, AND MODERATE-INCOME RENTALS

This is the story of English-inspired Arts and Crafts house designs for three classes of people on the lower rungs of the Massachusetts social system: servants; working class families primarily associated with employment by a transportation company; and working to lower-middle-class Salem residents displaced by the terrible 1914 fire that made whole neighborhoods uninhabitable. These are groups that did not ordinarily have access to architect-designed housing: only special circumstances and wealthy patrons made it possible.

Those houses constructed for the builders' own servants reflected the owners' notion of themselves as the inheritors of a benevolent Anglo-Saxon aristocratic tradition. The workers housing project, by contrast, was constructed by wealthy philanthropists for working families who had little connection to the benefactors who initiated it.[1] That project also had an English model, but the decision-makers did not adopt its total planned community framework. The third group, the Salem houses, were funded by a single philanthropic Salem resident for people needing moderate-income housing, replaced closely spaced, poorly built wooden tenements with neat, low, double houses in fireproof concrete.

⊰ Servants' Cottages ⊱

Massachusetts retains three examples of Arts and Crafts style servants' housing built between 1905 and 1912, during the last years of the Gilded Age, when great wealth was concentrated in the hands of a few families who sometimes displayed it in vast, splendid houses and extravagant entertainment. Perhaps not coincidentally, 1912 was the year the first United States Federal income tax was making its way through state ratification. Of the three examples, only the Eames family chose to forgo the grand mansion and invest their inherited wealth in a rambling but relatively modest house. It was, however, set in a grand and enviable landscape created from many accumulated parcels of land and landscaped by a master. The Eames family's houses in Boston on Commonwealth Avenue and Prides Crossing in Beverly were more spectacular.

Servants' cottages necessarily concern both the owner and the servant, but since we know much more about the former than the latter, we will have to allow the servants for whom the cottages were built a dignified but anonymous state while concentrating on their masters. House servants typically lived in the owner's house, either on another floor than used by the family or, if on the same floor, in an area with its own bathroom, isolated by a door and serviced by back stairs used only by the help. Specialized servants such as laundresses or dressmakers might come in for the day, but wealthy owners preferred their servants to live in the house. However, head gardeners and chauffeurs, who had superior social standing to that of most house servants, often had wives and so were occasionally housed in the specially constructed, architect-designed buildings on the property.

All three examples were built on or near the country estates of the owner: two were two-family double houses, another for a single family. Much of their significance lies in the fact that, while the master's house of the period was designed in an inflated form of the Colonial Revival or Italian Renaissance style, those for employees were executed in English-inspired Arts and Crafts. Clearly, that style was thought suitable for the higher of the lower classes, picturesque rather than elegant, charming rather than impressive, and substantially built, as befitted a building on the estate of an American patrician.

Henry Clay Frick's Gardner's Cottage, Eagle Rock Estate, Prides Crossing, Beverly

As a critic writing in 1912 observed, New Englanders tended to build their large country houses with sobriety and restraint "but if a country place becomes too big and handsome and pretentious . . . its owner is usually a Western millionaire."[2] This is essentially true of "Eagle Rock," Henry Clay Frick's summer house in the exclusive, summer house neighborhood of Prides Crossing in Beverly. Frick grew up not in the West but forty miles from Pittsburgh in western Pennsylvania and maintained a mansion in Pittsburgh while his palatial home in New York City, now the Frick Museum, contained his superb art collection. The 104-room Massachusetts house he built in 1904 is as large and ornate as Arthur Little[3] and Herbert Browne, its architects, could make it: a gaudy mix of Colonial Revival, Neo-Classical, and Beaux Arts styles in white-trimmed brick. The mansion was set on a hilltop site of twenty-five acres overlooking the Atlantic amidst terraced gardens designed by the Olmstead Brothers and surrounded by a large engine house, power house, and vast stable. The main house was demolished in 1969 at Frick's daughter's request: it was simply too large to maintain, even though one wing had been previously demolished as a cost-saving measure.

Frick (1849–1919) amassed his wealth in the wildly developing steel industry as the material became the choice for tall buildings, factories, warehouses, and warships. He previously controlled much of the market in the coke used in the production of steel. In 1889 Frick was made chairman of Carnegie Steel Company, then the largest manufacturer of the product in the world, and in 1901 director of the United States Steel Company he helped to form. His role in breaking the bloody, national-front-page Homestead strike and busting the union that supported it in 1892 led to an assassination attempt on his life. The strike would have a lasting effect on labor/capital relations.

In contrast to the brutal treatment of his steelworker

employees, Frick provided excellent accommodations for the employees on his Beverly estate. His gardener's cottage by the same architects (Figure 5.1) exhibits a playful facility, echoing the imagery of Pennsylvania's vernacular vocabulary such as the use of stone and an ingenious variation of the pent roof but with a subtle English Arts and Crafts sensibility. The one-and-one-half-story structure was designed with an unusual ground floor pass-through between two quite asymmetrical units that remained connected on the upper floor. The opening between them leading to the tennis courts behind the cottages has since been closed and a door installed to unify the units as a single-family dwelling. The original entries to the units were located in the passageway, a method of allowing their façades to directly hug the ground.

Unusual for a servants' house is the complicated roofline and the use of rough, random coursed fieldstone for the ground floor. Contrasting with the stuccoed upper floor is the dark red-brown granite of the ashlar quoins and a bright red slate roof that knits together the whole. Dominating each unit are oversized jerkin-head cross gables with extra deep, sheltering eaves that are terminated at the bottom with pent roofs supported on wooden brackets. These roofs, a feature of both Pennsylvania and Massachusetts domestic architecture, overhang the ground floor bay windows that serve each unit. A tall exterior chimney uses the same dark stone as the quoins while three other chimney tops are elaborated with corbelling. Little and Browne's composition fits these elements tightly together but looks easy and welcoming. Perhaps it is so carefully designed because Frick occupied it during the construction of his mansion up the hill.

In the original plan, the smaller unit to the right of the passage labeled the Annex, had only a "Main Room" with a corner hearth, an unfinished attic above, and a "Trunk Room" in the second-floor link. An undated but probably revised plan located a dining room in the attic and a kitchen in the link to the larger unit. The much roomier main unit contained a hall, living and dining rooms, kitchen, four bedrooms, bathroom, and a laundry in the basement. It was carefully detailed with a built-in dresser, cupboards, cabinets, and space for covered flour barrels in the kitchen, a storage bench in the hall, turned bannisters on the stair, and closets in the bedrooms.[4] Both units had covered piazzas with diamond-patterned trellises supporting the roof, a well-designed amenity. Frick opened his checkbook for this showpiece: according the architect's account book, the double cottage cost an astounding $18,902.82. Since the cost of a small, single-family house for a middle-class family in 1915 was estimated to be about $5,000: for this amount Frick could have built three-and-one-half ordinary houses.[5]

The estate's extensive frontage was enclosed by an extravagantly expensive, ornate cast iron fence anchored by stone posts topped with large stone balls.[6] The Gardener's Cottage, visible through a secondary opening, is placed to recall an English gate lodge, playing its role in projecting

FIGURE 5.1 506 Hale Street, Beverly (Little & Browne, 1904). A close look at the ground floor stonework reveals the butting together of two traditions: the random-coursed, rough fieldstone walls are in the vernacular idiom, while the dressed, squared-off sandstone quoins marking the house's corners and original central opening are in the classical tradition.

ARTS AND CRAFTS HOUSING FOR SERVANTS, WORKERS, AND MODERATE-INCOME RENTALS

FIGURE 5.2 23 Wellesley Street, Weston (Harold S. Graves, ca. 1910). The one-and-one-half story house is sited on a downslope from the street and set low to the ground, giving it a cottage-like appearance. Note the overhanging eaves had to be cut back to accommodate the tiny leaded glass oriel whose diamond panes are proportional to its size.

an Anglophile imagery.[7] The fence proved critical in August of 1912, when Mr. and Mrs. Frick gave a party for four hundred "beautifully gowned" socialites who strolled "acre after acre of velvet lawns."[8] They were served lunch and supper and were entertained by John Phillips Sousa's band and a concert by Frick's private organist. The New York Times reported a scene that had provoked unparalleled local excitement: "Thousands gathered outside the big iron and stone fence surrounding the estate, but had to be content with a view of the people as they whizzed through the gates in motor cars."[9]

⊰ Horace S. Sears's Estate Manager's House, Weston ⊱

Horace S. Sears erected a servant's cottage on his property at 23 Wellesley Street in Weston in about 1910, eight years after his own mansion was completed (Figure 5.2). It is thought to have been built for his estate manager or head gardener. Sears grew up in Weston, the son of the minister of its First Parish Church who wrote the lyrics of "It Came Upon a Midnight Clear."

With a partner, Sears made his fortune in industrial textiles produced in Alabama mills. Although he commuted to Boston on the nearby Central Massachusetts Rail Road, he was enormously fond of his hometown and its great benefactor, devoting his energy and money to projects that would enhance it—gifts to the schools, a new First Parish Church (1930), a library, the Town Green, and a new Town Hall, named for him. He was enamored of the theater and a member of the First Parish Church's amateur theatrical group, for whom he commissioned a 200-seat theater as one of the wings of his ornate Italianate style house. Designed by the usually more restrained Joseph Everett Chandler and set on an estate of fifty-six acres, the mansion was landscaped with immaculate gardens, terraces, and pools by the Olmsted Brothers and Arthur Shurtleff. It was erected about 1909 to reflect Sear's desire for "something stamped with the badge of success."[10] The house had a great hall with marble pillars capped by golden filigree, a library with tooled leather walls, and a sunken bath. A Weston resident remembered "Horace Sears got rich quick and his taste showed it!"[11] Sears purchased the top of Pigeon Hill in Weston, had the Olmsted Brothers subdivide it and lay out their signature curvilinear streets, then sold the lots to business and professional men. The servant's house was not in the high-class subdivision but in an area of tradesmen and workers for the three large estates nearby. It and an adjacent house for another Sears employee were located on the fringes of his estate.

Although Sears gave generously to Weston schools, he was not nearly as solicitous of the children employed in his southern mills. He and his partner did erect a church, Sunday School, worker housing, and an elementary school, as was usual in paternalistic southern textile mill villages. But in hiring children between the ages of six and twelve for eight or twelve hours a day, he badly undercut any chance for them to gain a real education. After a group of clerics, school superintendents, state legislators, and others formed the Alabama Child Labor Committee to repeatedly introduce reform legislation, Massachusetts mill owners hired lobbyists to oppose them. In response to this outside interference, Rev. Edgar Murphy, chair of the local committee, published an appeal addressed to the "people and press of New England," asking their "help in relation to the increasing evils of child labor. . . ."[12]

Murphy believed that Massachusetts citizens, having a state law outlawing employment of those under the age fourteen, would naturally question Alabama's "heartless policy" for those under twelve.[13] In this he was mistaken. Horace Sears belittled Murphy's argument, in spite of the fact that he agreed that child labor was wrong and, moreover, caused losses to the mills. Fearing that parents might move elsewhere to gain the meager wages their children could bring in, he would continue to actively oppose protective legislation.

Weston resident Harold S. Graves, the architect responsible for the estate manager's house, had designed a theater wing addition for the 1902 Sears mansion. The wood-shingled estate manager's house, while not clad in stucco, clearly betrays its Arts and Crafts identification in a number of gestures. The most prominent feature is the deeply overhanging false thatched slate roof ending in a steep catslide towards the original corner of the house.[14] Graves added to the romantic cottage's English appearance through the banked casement windows with large, diamond-shaped panes and unusually wide lead fastening strips, pointed rafter tails, and shutters with cutouts of a flower in a pot. A broad, stucco chimney on the façade thrusts through the peak of the cross gable. The offset entry is marked by an arched hood on brackets: its curving shape, suggestive of the Colonial Revival style, can be found in variations of English Arts and Crafts work.

⌁ Oliver Ames's "Twin Cottages," for the Servants of Sheep Pasture Estate, Easton, (also known as the Hafstrom-Swanson House) ⌁

Oliver Ames II (1864–1929), the owner of the cottages shown in Figure 5.3, was a scion of a remarkably talented family that claimed Mayflower passengers and later made fortunes in the manufacture of the humble shovel. The first Oliver Ames (born 1779) was a blacksmith who tinkered with shovels, moved to Easton, Massachusetts, in 1803, and set up a shop manufacturing iron shovels. The next Ames generation improved on these by making them in steel and a shape more suited to New England soil than English imports. These shovels were well-shaped, light, and reasonably priced. Acknowledged as the tool that opened the American West, the shovel was carried by almost every westward settler and American and Australian Gold Rush participant.

The Ames family grew richer during the Civil War when President Lincoln personally asked the company to supply shovels to the Union troops. Oliver's sons, Oakes and Oliver Jr., continued the growing shovel business in Easton and became essential in the development of the transcontinental railroad. Oliver was actually president of the railroad when workmen drove in the golden spike connecting eastward and westward rail lines. Oliver's son, Frederick Lothrop Ames (1835–1893), said to be the wealthiest man in Massachusetts, became a major philanthropist, donating a unique collection of H. H. Richardson's buildings to the town of Easton.

Frederick's son, Oliver, who commissioned the Twin Cottages, followed his father as the president and treasurer of the shovel shop. Oliver and his wife commissioned Frederick Law Olmsted to design the landscaping on a large piece of land in Easton, and society architects Rotch and Tilden to design a house (1903) they named Sheep Pasture. The house was demolished in 1946 but much of its acreage was donated to a land trust in Easton.

To design the double cottage for Sheep Pasture estate servants, Oliver and Elise chose the architects Parker and Thomas who in 1905 had designed the nearby Colonial Revival style mansion of Frederick Lothrop Ames. That fifty-room brick pile, located across the street from the cottages, is now the signature building of Stonehill College. Before the erection of the Twin Cottages, a simple vernacular Cape Cod cottage built in the 1860s stood on the lot. It became the home of a family that farmed and cared for the pigs at Sheep Pasture estate. When Oliver and Elise decided to build a new cottage to house their higher-status greenhouse gardener and chauffeur, the modest house was moved to an empty lot around the corner, leaving a large lot for the new, more stylish cottages.

The firm of Parker and Thomas was well established in Massachusetts and in Baltimore, Thomas' hometown, with dozens of houses and buildings to its credit. J. Harlston Parker and Douglas J. Thomas were MIT graduates and had studied at the Ecole des Beaux-Arts: Arthur W. Rice joined the partnership in 1907, seven years after it was established. Parker was later so concerned with the state of architecture in that in 1921, through the Boston Society of Architects and the City of Boston, he funded a yearly Parker medal for the single most beautiful building or structure built in Boston or the Metropolitan Park District over the preceding ten years.[15]

Like Frick's servants' cottage, Ames's double cottage consists of two joined units, each with a front gable, end porch, and rear ell. It is set facing south on a flat terraced area leading down to an extensive lawn. Historic photographs such as the one in Figure 5.4 show steps down to the greensward with an arched trellis over a graveled center path and wide flower borders showing the handiwork of the estate's gardener.

A local historian described the cottages simply as "thatched," pointing out her primary impression of the structure, although it was roofed in asphalt. The rolled eaves seem to go on and on, protruding forward from the

FIGURE 5.3 "Twin Cottages" (Hafstrom-Swanson House), 359 Washington Street, Easton (Parker, Thomas and Rice, 1912). Originally wood shingled, the roof was made more bulbous when a new asphalt roof was installed over the old, as seen here when compared to the early, undated photograph of the house in Figure 5.4. A garden shed to the left of the house is set back from it.

FIGURE 5.4 "Twin Cottages" (Hafstrom-Swanson House), 359 Washington Street, Easton (Parker, Thomas and Rice, 1912). Early twentieth century photo of the cottages and garden. The garden was planned as an essential component of the site. Note the open casements of the center dormer and a man lounging in the right-hand doorway.

plane of the house, dipping low over the first-floor windows at the center, and making a final, long catslide over the cottage at the western end. To add to the thatched effect, the gable peaks, jerkin-heads over the attic windows, and shed-roofed dormers are also rounded.[16] The green-painted trellises surrounding the front doors and the window boxes are still in place.

The cottages were differentiated by varying the details. The easternmost has a rolled pent roof over the door, possibly unique in America, and a bay window. It originally had a porch set back from the façade with a large rectangular front and side openings, now replaced with a one-story addition. The western unit featured an oriel window and a long catslide roof curving over its originally open porch. Placed close to the road but fronting a large garden space, the cottages were carefully designed to provide a picturesque image of the estate's retainers in their Arcadian sophistication. Descendants of servants continued to live in the two houses until it was purchased in 1980 and subsequently renovated to house Stonehill College's President.

⊰ Worker's Housing: Woodbourne: Housing for Trolley Workers and Their Families ⊱

In the nineteenth and early twentieth centuries, Massachusetts factory owners often erected rental housing for their employees on company property. Repetitive in design, set on grids of streets, and clustered near the mill or factory, these groups of company housing still dot the rural landscape. They also erected boarding houses for single men and women operatives and, in a few cases, middle-class suburban single-family houses for the higher echelons of company administration. In 1909 a novel project by an idealistic real estate development company proposed an entirely different model. It would provide modest homes, not for rent but for sale to workers at prices they could afford, located outside the city but made easily accessible by inexpensive and frequent public transportation. Boston's Woodbourne survives as a reminder of the aspirations and failures of this reformist group whose actions turned their good intentions into tangible housing.

⊰ The Background ⊱

In 1820, Boston's population stood at 43,298 almost entirely native-born people, but in the three decades that followed, the city's population more than tripled, with almost half being foreign born. Low-cost housing had not been built fast enough to accommodate the influx of steadily arriving poor immigrants and workers from surrounding states and abroad. In the 1880s, the high rate of city taxes on improvements to tenement houses discouraged the maintenance of, and investment in, the cheaply built buildings. By the 1890s, densely packed slums made the problem of housing the poor a topic of ardent debate among the city's wealthy, civic-minded citizens.

They were concerned about fire prevention in the closely spaced and rickety wooden tenements; the severe overcrowding that saw three to five families crammed into one unit, people sleeping in shifts on the floors; a lack of sufficient light, air, and ventilation on the constricted lots; the fetid alleys between the buildings; and the terrible sanitation where one toilet sometimes served multiple families. Boston's Anti-Tenement League forcefully pointed out that, due to the then-current garment-making sweatshop system, very small, ill-lit, and unventilated rooms were often sixteen-hour worksites as well as cooking and sleeping chambers.

Various Massachusetts laws attempted to insure better fire safety such as an 1871 Boston building code that limited wooden buildings in the center of the city, although not at its fast-growing edges. Data on the poor living conditions and public health issues, such as unconscionably high child mortality and tuberculosis in slum districts, had been collected by the state since 1891 but action to remediate them were not yet thought to be the province of government. The state edged towards a more active involvement in providing more and better housing for the poor with the establishment of a Homestead Commission in 1911 and the passage of a Tenement Reform Act in 1912–1913 that allowed cities to prohibit the construction of frame three-deckers. This phenomenally popular house form of three floors, generally each with a small porch, contained one or sometimes more units on each floor. Architects and civic-minded residents however, condemned the usually densely built buildings as tawdry firetraps of shoddy construction.[17]

Because state and municipal governments fell shy of taking responsibility to construct more and better housing for the poor, it was mainly left to the public citizenry, under the banner of reform movements, to bring deplorable conditions to the notice of the voters, encourage government involvement, and occasionally undertake an experimental development. To respond to these distressing conditions, a group called "Boston 1915" incorporated in 1909 to devise a plan for the future of their city. Led by wealthy reformers like Edward A. Filene, Boston's major department store owner; Louis D. Brandeis, "the people's lawyer" and later Supreme Court justice; and James T. Storrow, an investment banker and philanthropist for whom Storrow Drive is named, it also included business leaders, labor unions, settlement house leaders, and the city's social service department. Boston 15's extremely popular exhibition and magazines brought substandard housing conditions "which demand radical remedy" to the attention of the city's public.[18]

⸙ The Boston Dwelling House Company ⸙

It was in this climate that the Boston Dwelling House Company was formed in 1909 to alleviate the dire situation of working men and their families. A brick trade journal described its purpose glowingly: "To combat this unhealthy state of affairs and to provide as an example for investors, a suburb which should be charming, picturesque, practical and a real asset to the city, improving and holding up values in its vicinity . . . , a company of some of the most far-seeing and public spirited men and women of Boston organized last year a strong corporation known as the Boston Dwelling House Company."[19] In one sentence the editorial linked, in a particularly American fashion, investors, real estate values, the charming, the picturesque, and the practical.

The company's first and most important project, Woodbourne, was located in Jamaica Plain's Forest Hills section of Boston. In the 1840s, Forest Hills was an accurate name—boasting wide views from tree-crowned hills. Not far from the city center, wealthy Bostonians like William Minot, a lawyer and judge, purchased land in 1845 and built a summer house high on a hill. With the opening of the Boston & Providence Railroad in 1834, the area had become accessible from the city. Minot's estate, called Woodbourne after the romantic home of a Sir Walter Scott character, was eventually surrounded by the year-round houses of his children and others. Forest Hills, annexed to Boston in 1874, underwent growing suburbanization and became a popular streetcar suburb when a more modern form of transportation, the West End Railway Company's electrified streetcar system, began service to the community in 1891.

Robert Winsor Jr., a wealthy, multitalented, and powerful investment banker at Boston's large, prestigious Kidder, Peabody and Co., was a director of Boston Elevated Railway Company, what we might today call light rail. In 1895, Winsor gained control of the West End Railway Company that owned much of the region's ground-level trolley and subway systems. The purchase and consolidation moved toward his goal of creating a unified public transit system, for public good and his firm's financial control of the metropolitan commuter market. In 1909, Winsor participated in the visionary Boston–1915 movement, naturally as chairman of its Transportation Committee.

Perhaps his chief civic interest was in alleviating Boston's housing problems, so much so that he became the animating force in creating The Boston Dwelling House Company and a director. The goal of the company was to erect low-cost workers' housing for sale at reasonable prices outside the congested city. Winsor gathered wealthy men, activist women, a settlement house advocate, and even Boston's Catholic Cardinal as Company directors. Henry Howard, the magnetic MIT graduate, chemical engineer, and businessman, led the organization as president, with Winsor's son Robert Jr., as Treasurer. Howard, whose Brookline home is pictured in Figure 2.1, was an MIT classmate of Walter H. Kilham, Woodbourne's principal architect.

Between 1909 and 1911, The Boston Elevated Railway Company built an elevated trolley station and maintenance car-barns in Forest Hills. Not coincidentally, in 1911, in his capacity as a director of the Boston Dwelling House Company, Winsor proposed to build on the recently available Minot property near the car-barns a "scientific, model residential enclave for its conductors and motormen as an alternative to the ills of urban housing and congestion."[20] The philanthropic but practical company evidently believed the conductors and motormen had sufficient salaries to afford to buy a house, if offered at a low enough price, and would wish to live near their workplace.

Housing reformers of the early twentieth century hopefully believed that home ownership was the antidote to the squalid and unhealthy tenements. It would engender middle-class ideals of probity, stability, and cleanliness. But since the private housing market could or would not build enough affordable homes, the nonprofit sector would be obliged to do so. This had traditionally been the province of charitable institutions, but the Boston Dwelling House Company would not act entirely from charitable motives. Instead, it would be run as a business, making a modest return on capital investment.

A sales pamphlet published by the company entitled "How to Own a Home: A Feasible Plan for Persons with Moderate Incomes" posited that 99 percent of American families longed to own a home but were thwarted by high prices caused by the retail method of homebuilding and selling, and mortgage payment schedules that required high down payments and large, infrequent payments. To avoid these problems, the company would build on a large scale and on easy terms of payment. Selling the improbable idea of home ownership to the working class, the upbeat publication mentioned only the benefits of owning a home: security, independence, joy, and pride.

The company proposed to address the problem of scale by using its capital to purchase thirty acres, to be subdivided into lots, and design services such as road layout, house siting, house design, and landscaping. With great foresight, the developer provided electric and telephone service in underground conduits as well as gas, sewerage, and water lines. The second problem related to the customer of moderate means: it was assumed that "small payments at frequent intervals are possibly comparatively easy to make"[21] while large, infrequent ones made it "impossible to buy a home and still be able to meet from the family purse the necessary daily living expenses."[22] Much of the pamphlet was devoted to text and tables explaining the easy payment plan and its advantage to renting a similar property.

Winsor was interested in the garden suburb idea and sent agents to England to report back on several designed for company workers. While the Boston Dwelling House Company balked at the cooperative landowning concept of the Garden Suburb movement, it wholehearted adopted others. These included the careful siting of every dwelling to allow good ventilation, views, and a small garden; the placement of abundant playgrounds in sight of each owner's kitchen window; common green spaces; the retention of shade trees and the naturalistic layout of the streets that curved around hills to avoid city-like grid patterns. Another touch more typical of a purely commercial suburban development was the erection of an architect-designed tennis club for the residents. It was intended to promote a sense of community and belonging.

Winsor, who was already working with the famous

Olmsted Brothers landscape firm on his own 472-acre estate in Weston, asked them to design the site plan and road layout of what would be the Woodbourne development. When the plan proved too expensive to execute while serving the mission of providing the best house for the least money, Winsor broke the contract, dismissed the firm, and hired Robert Anderson Pope, a New York landscape architect and experienced town planner. Pope, a believer in the garden suburb objectives, retained a similar topographically sensitive road layout, attention to views, mature trees, and playgrounds, but grouped the housing clusters closer together than in the Olmsted plan. Cost-cutting was achieved by widening the through roads, narrowing those that were exclusively residential and reusing the fill removed from the apartment building sites for landscape improvements elsewhere.

Walter H. Kilham and James Hopkins were responsible for two Brookline Arts and Crafts style upper-class houses in this study[23] as well as many suburban houses, school buildings, and churches. Kilham was also intensely interested in the problem of housing the working man's family. After graduating from MIT he won the coveted Rotch fellowship that allowed him to travel extensively in Europe. He settled in Brookline, where he designed his own stucco home, and served on its planning board under the leadership of Fredrick Law Olmsted Jr. Kilham's strong dislike of the rickety three-decker apartment buildings built by the thousands in Massachusetts, desire to find a better model for housing working class families, and acquaintance with his MIT classmate, Boston Dwelling House Company president Henry Howard, got the firm the job of Woodbourne's chief designers. Kilham became an expert in low-cost housing and went on to design model working class houses in Salem after its devastating fire in 1914, and in Lowell, Brookline, and Portsmouth, New Hampshire.

Kilham was also eager to learn from the Garden City experiments taking place in England, visiting two company-built villages. His guide at Letchworth Garden City and Hampstead Garden Suburb was Raymond Unwin, a co-designer of both. Kilham thought of the company towns as paternalistic and Hampstead, intended for a white-collar clientele, as irrelevant to solving the social problem of housing the working class in the United States. Kilham's partner James C. Hopkins, another MIT graduate, spent part of every year in England and was deeply appreciative of its Arts and Crafts domestic architecture. Around 1910 he designed his own stucco house in Dover, Massachusetts, a large Arts and Crafts country estate with gunroom and servants' dining room, named a quintessentially English "Wychwood."

⊰ The Houses ⊱

Like the architects of England's garden suburbs, Woodbourne's architects aimed for picturesque groupings of single-family, two-family, and row housing types, but they also included six now demolished apartment buildings to buffer the houses from a busy street at the development's edge. As they were demolished in 1977, these larger buildings will not be discussed here. Given a modest budget, the simplified Arts and Crafts style of Woodbourne's houses needed to derive their appeal principally from their vernacular shapes. In speaking of the few simple decorative embellishments, the sales pamphlet reported "some of the houses have a portion of the gable in half-timbering, as the old English style."[24] In the end, only four of the single-family houses had this type of embellishment.

Aside from the apartment buildings, the goal was to achieve a measure of variety within a visually coherent system and to minimize design and materials costs. This was a departure from the English garden suburb practice: Port Sunlight is described as having many different styles while Letchworth's 1904 building regulations called only for "Simple and straightforward building with 'the use of good and harmonious materials,'" and discouraged "'useless ornamentation'."[25] Another departure from English practice was Woodbourne's location, not a truly rural environment chosen for its healthy air, recreational purposes, and space for industrial use, but located not far from the trolley barns in a fast-growing suburb a five-cent fare away from the city on a trolley that ran every five minutes.

All the development's houses had sea-green slate roofs, producing an appearance of unity and permanence. Kilham & Hopkins' original plans called for stucco cladding—over rectangular blocks of hollow tile for the larger houses and frame for the smaller ones. But on hearing this, J. Parker Fiske, a Boston brick manufacturer and the secretary of the Building Brick Association of America, and a builder, Arthur W. Joslyn, determined to mount a protest for the use of brick. The latter had just published a book enumerating the construction costs of brick versus stucco houses showing the relative finished prices of each technique. Fiske had recently patented a new, rough-textured brick he called "Tapestry" that was intended to be laid in a mix of colors.

The two men "went to the President of the Boston Dwelling House Company and the architects, Alham [sic] & Hopkins and showed them why they should consider brick."[26] Joslyn may have made a convincing argument on the issue of savings with his detailed financial data on the comparative prices of building in brick, which was only fractionally more expensive than stucco but had better durability. Fiske, an MIT graduate,[27] had an aesthetic argument as he had earlier claimed that his signature product was "to ordinary brick what Arts and Crafts furniture is to the gilt and velvet of the last century."[28] They must have been convincing, as two groups of twelve houses each were erected in red-brown tapestry brick with white trim. The company's sales brochure opined that the brick gave a "very pleasing soft color effect."[29]

Every dwelling in the development was equipped with a porch, however small, for outdoor socializing. The scheme offered three classes of houses. The first was largest and had a living room with fireplace and mantle, dining

FIGURE 5.5 . Florian Island houses, center oval, Boston (Kilham & Hopkins, 1912–1913). Right: 296 Wachusett Street, 96R Florian Street, and 92 Florian Street. Left: 98R Florian Street and 25 Southbourne Road. These houses have been much altered with in-filled porches, non-original trim, and additional windows, but it is still possible to see their intimate arrangement due to the absence of road frontage and the rhythm established by the alternating orientation of the gables.

room, and kitchen. The upper floor of these one-and-one-half-story houses contained either three or four bedrooms and a bathroom. Some kitchen pantries were fitted with under-counter barrels that swung outwards for storing flour, a convenience for housewives with small budgets before sliced bread became widely available in markets. Hardwood floors, enameled or papered walls, shades, copper screens, and either basement or kitchen washtubs were standard, as were glazed built-in china cupboards in the dining rooms.

In an innovative layout, Pope and the architects located ten one-and-one-half story cottages on a pointed oval formed by intersecting roads. In the wide middle area, they set two rows of three gambrel-roofed houses facing each other across a center pedestrian path, with walks off it to each house. Although small, this greenspace acted as a visual common. Each house had an inset porch, most of which have since been filled to gain interior space (see Figure 5.5). The houses alternated front and side gables: those in the center had entries sheltered by a balustrade-topped portico and those at row's end were entered through an inset porch trimmed with trellis work.[30] (See Figure 5.6.)

A pair of slightly more ornamented single-family houses were sited at each end of the oval. Also executed in hollow tile and stucco, they gain their distinctive shape from the jerkin-head or clipped gable roofs, and style from the

FIGURE 5.6 . Florian Island houses, center oval, Boston (Kilham & Hopkins, 1912–1913). Boston Dwelling House Company promotion photo taken soon after the houses were erected showing intact original form, trim, and landscaping.

FIGURE 5.7 . 90 Florian Street, Boston (Kilham & Hopkins, 1912). A drawing and plan of this house type appeared in the marketing brochure showing the living room and dining room with a wide opening between them so that each could borrow visual space from the other. The two larger and one small bedrooms and bath upstairs may have been intended for a smaller family.

half-timbering that appears in the gable field and around the hip-roofed dormers thrusting through the eaves. A deep string-course encircles these houses to visually set off the upper from the first floor, making the cottages appear slightly larger than their actual one-and-one-half stories. The example shown in Figure 5.7 retains the shutters that were standard on the oval.

Kilham & Hopkins originally designed the assemblage of two identical groups of twelve dwellings in hollow tile and stucco, but they were ultimately executed in brick following Fiske and Joslyn's persuasive visit. Set well back from the road and fronting an extensive lawn, the center-piece of each was a six-unit block of row houses with their distinctive jerkin-head and catslide roofs. It was diagonally flanked by a side-gable double and a single-family cottage on each side (Figure 5.8). In the sales brochure, the architects pointed out these groups were sited in a "compact arrangement which, at the same time, gives the greatest possible privacy surrounded as the block is by parks."[31] By parks the author meant the open areas between the dwellings and the street.

The two groups of six semidetached houses, were the sole such type planned for the development and remain the only ones in the Boston Dwelling House Company's Woodbourne property. Their open U-shape created a small courtyard, as the architects stated "very much in the form of those built in England today."[32] The imaginative planning, in placing the space-saving row-houses at the apex of the flanking one and two-family cottages, made them appear not only as the culmination of a graduated ensemble but also appear less urban as placed amongst the cottages on the wide green setting. The innovative grouping also meant that, although they occupied the same amount of space as an equal number of units of three-deckers sited six feet apart would have contained, these were located at spacious twenty-five-foot intervals. The siting scheme con-

FIGURE 5.8 30–52 Southbourne Street, Boston (Kilham & Hopkins, 1912). Care was taken to site the houses so as to retain the hilltop views and mature trees on the property. The now-enclosed porches were originally open for air and sociability.

flicted with Boston's building law, but the architects wrote that it was warmly approved.[33]

Another group of houses was designed by the architectural firm of Allen and Collens. Francis Allen (1843–1931) and his younger colleague, Charles Collens (1873–1956), the lead architects for this group, had both studied at MIT and the École des Beaux-Arts and were a well-established firm with dozens of houses and college buildings to their credit. Collens is most famous for his later design for the Cloisters in New York City. The firm also designed the Woodbourne Club building in rustic fieldstone and its two tennis courts.

Allen and Collens were responsible for only one group of small, ultra-low-cost dwellings at Woodbourne. The three starter houses containing four units were planned for newlyweds or small families. Of cheaper construction than the others, they were neither as large nor as fireproof as the stucco-parged hollow tile or brick cottages, as they were constructed in frame covered with stucco. Marking

FIGURE 5.9 80–82 Southbourne Road, Boston (Allen and Collens, 1913). Although the porch on the left of this two-family house is now enclosed, this group of three small buildings has suffered less from unfortunate alterations than have many of the larger houses.

these dwellings as the work of a different architectural firm are the unusual mansard roofs having a shallow upper and deep lower slope, the single examples in the development. Consequently, these cottages relate to the rest of the Boston Dwelling House Company houses primarily by their stucco finish and green-slated roofs, although deep, lid-like roofs may qualify as an Arts and Crafts gesture.

    The group is composed of a two-family semidetached house set well back from the street (Figure 5.9) flanked by two single-family houses to form a rough U shape. The generous open space in front acted as a common yard (see Figure 5.10). Each of the four units in this group had the

FIGURE 5.10 84 Southbourne Road. Allen and Collens, 1912. One of two identical cottages, the porch trellises, brackets, oriel window and arched pediment topping the entries might have been intended as recompense for the cottage's tight internal spaces. .

same interior plan: in the two-family attached house, the plan on one side was simply reversed to mirror the other. The tiny dwellings had no entry hall: one stepped from a covered porch directly into the living room. To conserve space, the dining room was omitted and the family ate in the kitchen. The second floor contained a bathroom, a small master bedroom, and an even smaller child's room. The second-floor chambers are lit by shed-roof dormers, placed on the façade for the double-family and on the side for the single-family houses.

⊰ The Development's Outcome ⊱

The landscape planner and project architects originally envisioned using much of Woodbourne's thirty acres. The curving streets would be built up with one hundred and twenty-seven single and double houses. It is not clear why only thirty-eight single-, double-, and six-family units were constructed. Building according to the published plans ceased about 1914. Perhaps this stoppage concerned the class of persons who actually purchased the houses: not the workers the Boston Dwelling House Company had expected but middle-managers, teachers, dentists, and salesmen. Inexpensive as the developers had tried to make them, the houses were simply too costly for the trolley and other workers for whom they were built. Additionally, the higher than expected finished cost of the dwellings certainly meant the company made less than the expected profit.[34] A depression and the intervention of World War I caused a halt to the housing market and the end of the carefully planned community. Ironically, architect Charles Collens bought for resale all four small-family houses his firm had designed, putting their low cost in jeopardy as he would have sold or rented them for his own gain.

Looking back, Walter Kilham believed the problem had been too many costly amenities such as fireplaces, furnaces, and piazzas, to say nothing of the wallpaper and window shades. On the other hand, he compared his houses to those of the English Letchworth Garden City stating, the "Letchworth house without cellar, closets, bathroom, electricity or furnace cost the equivalent of . . . 15 cents per cubic foot, while the Boston houses, also built of brick with slated roof, containing all these amenities, cost no more and were better."[35]

After the war, the Boston Dwelling House Company sold off the remaining lots to individuals without regard to the original idealistic plans. The street layouts remain but the houses erected after 1914 have no relationship to each other or to community open spaces. Failure to realize the dream of high-quality worker housing by charitable or limited-profit companies was the plight of the few such low-income projects undertaken in the early twentieth century. It would take state and federal acceptance of responsibility for housing the economically vulnerable to advance towards that goal, a responsibility both Massachusetts residents and government officials were slow to meet, though the need was evident to most.

⊰ Affordable Housing: Rebuilding After Salem's Great Fire of 1914–Orne Square ⊱

The historic city of Salem's terrible fire of 1914 began in mid-June of 1914 in a sheepskin factory located in the aptly named Blubber Hollow. It spread quickly, burning an area of 251 acres, a half-mile wide and over a mile long, consuming 1,792 buildings and leaving 15,000 people homeless. The disaster called for prompt action and the Commonwealth rose to meet it: in early July, the Massachusetts Legislature created the Salem Rebuilding Commission with extraordinary powers and a three-year term. One of its first acts was the appointment of Clarence H. Blackhall, a distinguished Boston architect known for his innovative theaters, apartment buildings, and tall, steel office buildings.

Since Salem's building code was rudimentary and outdated, Blackhall quickly created a new one that attempted to balance the need for immediate rebuilding, so that the affected residents might soon return, with the need for increased fire protection regulations that might, however, slow the building process. Blackhall attempted to convince builders to use reinforced concrete as a fireproof material but wrote "The idea that the City should build or directly formulate the plans for private building is so foreign to the idea of an American city or town that it could not be accepted here, notwithstanding the terrible lesson of the fire."[36] Further analyzing Salem residents' aversion to exterior control, Blackhall found that "the American people do not care for collective building, but would rather preserve their individual ideas and freedom of action even at an increased cost."[37]

The new building code prohibited wooden three-deckers outright. It required new, multifamily buildings to institute certain fire-protective measures, including more space around buildings, and barring wood roofs. But buildings housing one or two families, such as those for modest rentals at Orne Square, could be built much as the owner wished.

Sarah Ropes Orne's will left the parcel of land that became Orne Square to Nathaniel Ropes V, her nephew, in 1876. Like that of so many of the town's upper-class residents, the wealth of the Ropes family, residents of a grand Georgian mansion (ca. 1727) on Salem's original main street, came from the China Trade. It was Nathaniel who, ten years later, erected closely spaced wooden tenements on the vacant land to house twenty-seven working-poor families. He named the development and street Orne Square for his aunt. After his death in 1893 the rental units were managed by a trust.

The fire of 1914 burned the 1886 tenements to the ground, though it spared the Ropes Mansion. Hoping to alleviate the grave housing crisis and perhaps improve an area previously occupied by flimsy, closely spaced wooden tenements, another rich woman stepped in. Mrs. Ann Maria Pingree Wheatland, the widow of a former Salem mayor, lived not far from the decimated Orne Square in a Colonial Revival mansion (1896) by Salem architect John L. Benson.[38] She secretly bought the Orne Square parcel from the trust and hired Ambrose Walker (1869–1967) a Boston architect who lived in Salem, to design the houses she would build there as moderate rental units.

Mrs. Wheatland knew Walker as the MIT classmate and architectural partner of Ernest Machado who had designed her summer house in Rangeley, Maine. After Machado's early death in a boating accident in 1907, Walker

120

FIGURE 5.11 Orne Square, Salem (Ambrose Walker, 1915-16). Photo taken circa 1925. Placing the houses at the sidewalk line allowed space for hidden gardens at the rear. The narrowness of the street and small number of identical cottages create a sense of village neighborliness.

became the architect of Rangeley's small but charming Arts and Crafts style 1909 Library, distinguished by its curving, false-thatched roofline. Wheatland made a happy choice in the selection of Walker as the architect of her development. He was deeply interested in designing housing for people of limited means, and was familiar with the concepts of community and planning that actuated the Garden Cities of England as well as its architecture, particularly the popular two-family semidetached house form. As

seen in his Rangeley Library, he was attracted to the Arts and Crafts style. Walker's houses and buildings are not well-documented so we know of only a few, but they wear well. As the critic of the period, Mary Northland, wrote of Walker's Orne Square group a few years after they were built, "The houses are artistic and comfortable, and the development worthy of being copied in any small city."[39]

Not literally a square, the eight double houses are laid out on both sides of an L-shaped street with their facades at

FIGURE 5.12 10–12 Orne Square, Salem, detail. The segmentally arched porches are graceful and announce the buildings' masonry construction. Residents have found ways of individuating their houses while maintaining a sense of the whole.

FIGURE 5.13 10–12 Orne Square, Salem (Ambrose Walker, 1915). This recent photograph shows how little these houses' exteriors have changed in the nearly one hundred years since they were constructed.

the sidewalk line.[40] (See Figure 5.11 and 5.13) Although not required to be fireproof by the building code, the houses were built of first-class materials for preventing fire damage: concrete block—unusual in architect-designed buildings but cheap and sturdy—coated with Portland cement, with slate roofs. Each house has a sheltered rear yard accessed from both house and sidewalk, while a small open space at the corner of the dog-leg was provided for common recreation.

Two stories and high attics with pitched roofs, buttered in the same colored stucco and minimally detailed, the group maintains a high level of quiet cohesion. The segmentally arched tops of the inset porches set up a pleasant rhythm and do much to relieve the repetition of a single uncluttered shape. The few ornaments—the plain, green-painted shutters and porch rails, balusters and window boxes are restrained but effective. The dwellings' intimate scale, simplicity of line, and pleasing relationship of solid to voids are suggestive of an English village (see Figure 5.12).

The first floor of each unit contains a small entry hall,

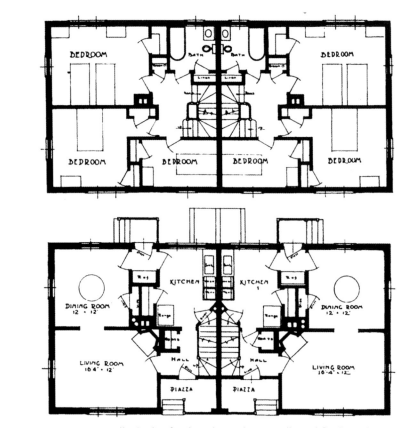

FIGURE 5.14 Walker's plan for these limited spaces allowed fluid circulation through the three first floor rooms, a homey catty-corner fireplace in the living room and direct access to the back yard.

living room with corner fireplace, dining room with built-in glassed cupboard and drawers, and kitchen (see plans in Figure 5.14). One smaller and two larger bedrooms, a bathroom and a linen closet are located on the second floor. It may have been Mrs. Wheatland who decided that every room in the house must have a door nearly opposite a window for ventilation. Lighting was also evidently important to owner and architect as the living rooms and master bedrooms are lit by paired, 6/6 windows on two elevations while two windows light the small kitchens. The multiple panes of the fenestration are an important contributor to the group's sense of scale.

Although the rooms are small, their proportions and abundant light make them cozy spaces. The cottages were soon rented by families of the class for whom they were built. In 1916 they housed a leatherworker, clerk, telegraph employee, foreman, salesman, lawyer, painter, baker, and cabinet worker. After Mrs. Wheatland's death, the property was managed by her son-in-law, and following his death, by a trust. The trust and later the owners of the now-cooperative units have maintained the group with care, so that not only the historic fabric but also the appearance of the sensitively designed ensemble has been preserved.

This group of houses shows what can be done with private money, a mission to provide moderate-income housing, and a sensitive design to craft not only livable interior and exterior spaces but also to create a development that makes the repetition of a single design a charming rather than a monotonous experience. Orne Square also demonstrates that, with skill, the humble, inexpensive construction material—concrete block—can be used to keep costs low but look highly attractive.

❧ Notes ❧

1 An exception was Robert Winsor who was both an executive of the Boston Elevated Railway trolley company and a leading activist in the creation of the Boston Dwelling House Company that built, sold, and financed housing intended primarily for the Boston Elevated trolley workers.

2 Herbert Croly, "The Work of Kilham & Hopkins," *The Architectural Review* XXI, no. 2 (February 1912).

3 Little was the father of J. Lovell Little Jr., the architect of 33 Circuit Road (see Figure 4.44), 43 Cottage Farm Road, and 105 Rockland Road (see Figure 4.27), all of Brookline.

4 See Plans of October 19, 1904 by Little and Browne at Historic New England Archive.

5 Ekin Wallick, *The Small House for a Moderate Income*. Of course, this double house was partly of masonry construction, which was more costly than the frame usual for this population.

6 When the iron railing surrounding the Gardener's Cottage area was removed for scrap metal for the World War II effort, the spaces between the columns were filled with wood paneling. Apparently, the iron never reached its intended destination but was retained and sold on the private market by the person hired to take it down. http://www.beyondthegildedage.com/2012/07/eagle-rock.html.

7 Plans and elevations for a large, highly decorated Gate Lodge in the Georgian style are found in the archives of Historic New England but it is probable that the building was never erected.

8 "H. C. Frick's Party Draws Thousands," *New York Times* (August 17, 1912).

9 Ibid.

10 Brenton H. Dickson, "Random Reflections," Diana Chaplin's Weston Real Estate website, https://www.greatestate.com/random-recollections/pages/86.php., 87.

11 Ibid.

12 Edgar Gardner Murphy, *Child Labor in Alabama: An Appeal to the People and Press of New England with a Resulting Correspondence.* (Montgomery, Alabama: Alabama Child Labor Committee, 1901), 3.

13 Ibid., 6

14   Owners added to the house on the north end, extending the slate roof and moving leaded-glass windows from the rear. (Pamela W. Fox, Massachusetts Historical Commission, Form B, Weston, Inventory #338, 1994).

15   In 2007 the area of eligibility for the Parker medal was extended to Greater Boston. Over the ninety-three years since winners were first selected (1923–2017) about seventy-two medals have been awarded.

16   The cottages, now converted to one, were recently reroofed with highly variegated, multicolored architectural shingle, making the roof more striking but less historically accurate. However, the original shingles remain under the new roof.

17   Ironically, due to the scarcity of housing in the early years of the twenty-first century Massachusetts made triple-deckers real estate prizes, ripe for expensive renovation and resale at inflated prices.

18   C. Bertrand Thompson. *New Boston: The Official Organ of Boston—1915* 1, no. 1 (Boston: May 1910), 10.

19   "Two Groups of Houses Built by the Boston Dwelling House Company," editorial in *The Brickbuilder* 22, no. 4 (April 1913), 93.

20   Greer Hardwick and Betsy Friedberg, "Woodbourne Historic District," as part of a nomination to the National Register of Historic Places (MA: Jamaica Plain Historical Society, 1999), http://www.jphs.org/locales/2004/1/1/woodbourne-historic-district.html.

21   Boston Dwelling House Company, *Woodbourne: A Real Estate Development of the Boston Dwelling House Company.* *"Woodbourne: A Description of Single and Semi-detached Houses Offered at This Attractive Site by the Boston Dwelling House Company, With Terms of Sale".* (MA: Jamaica Plain, 1912 and 1913), 7, https://babel.hathitrust.org/cgi/pt?id=uc1.31175011183111;view=1up;seq=15.

22   Ibid., 3.

23   The Kilham & Hopkins houses are located in Brookline at 474 Chestnut Hill Avenue (1915) with a "false thatched" roof, and 91 Seaver Street (1912) with half-timbered gables and squat stucco columns.

24   Boston Dwelling House Company, *Woodbourne*, 20.

25   Mervyn Miller, *English Garden Cities* (Swindon: 2010), 20. Miller quotes Raymond Unwin, "Building Regulations" reprinted in C. B. Purdon's *The Garden City: A Study in the Development of a Modern Town* (London: Dent, 1913). Much of Letchworth Garden City is in architect-designed Arts and Crafts style, while in Hampstead Garden Suburb, the houses are primarily Georgian Revival.

26   *Brick and Clay Record* (March 1913), 330.

27   MIT graduates Kilham (1889) and Fiske (1891) seem to have forged a bond, as it was probably Kilham who invited the brickmaker to his MIT class reunion, which enthusiastically adjourned to Fiske's offices to view his tapestry brick exhibit.

28   J. Parker Fiske, "Trademark 'Tapestry'," *Tapestry Brickwork* (Boston: Fiske and Co., Inc., 1912), 17–18.

29 Boston Dwelling House Company, *Woodbourne*, 20.

30 The houses are located, reading from the left and moving clockwise: 98R Florian, 25 Southbourne, 94 Florian, 96R Florian, and 296 Wachusett Streets.

31 Boston Dwelling House Company, *Woodbourne*, 10.

32 & Hopkins, "Two Groups of Houses Built for the Boston Dwelling House Company," *The Brickbuilder* 22, no. 4 (February 1913).

33 This siting scheme, modeled on the clustered housing of the English garden cities, was a very early introduction of the concept in the United States. The adoption of cluster zoning was still encountering suburban resistance in Massachusetts as late as the 1990s.

34 To keep costs at a minimum, the half-timbering originally shown in the gables of a group of brick two-family houses by Kilham & Hopkins for the Salem Rebuilding Commission was abandoned, considerably reducing their charm but increasing their profitability. Those cottages also dispensed with furnaces and dining rooms.

35 Greer Hardwick and Betsy Friedberg, "Woodbourne Historic District" National Register Nomination Form (1999).

36 "Report of the Advisory Architect to the Salem Rebuilding Commission," *Report of the Salem Building Commission* (Salem, Massachusetts: Newcomb and Gauss, Printers, 1917), 20, http://digitalcommons.salemstate.edu/cgi/viewcontent.cgi?article=1002&context=fire_documents.

37 Ibid., 4.

38 Benson probably designed the house in Salem built in the burned district at 76–78 Endicott Street (see Figure 4.14).

39 Mary H. Northend. *House Beautiful* (September 1920). Quoted in Donna Seger's *The Streets of Salem* blog, "An Urban Village in Salem", https://streetsofsalem.com/2016/09/05/an-urban-village-in-salem/.

40 The houses are located at 1–3, 2–4, 5–7, 6–8, 9–11, 10–12, 14–16, and 15–17 Orne Square.

Words make a very loosely woven net we throw over an idea to try to give it some shape. Simplicity and charm are words frequently used by the Massachusetts architects whose work is illustrated and by the critics quoted in this book. But both the image conveyed by the building and the statements about them are open to changing tastes and public understanding of the words. What is "simple" to one period often seems fussy to the following generation: what is "honest" might be read as disingenuous, "charming" as sentimental. The problem is particularly true in the twentieth-century America of rapidly transforming conditions and styles that shifted to express new circumstances.

Now that almost a century has passed between the erection of these houses and the present, we are ready to see them anew. They are no longer merely old-fashioned or sentimental but authentic expressions of a hopeful and idealistic period, of people looking to English tradition, but, as reinterpreted by Massachusetts architects, seeking to reintroduce the quality of hominess and unpretentiousness in their dwellings and to incorporate an artistic way of designing living spaces. These houses deserve attention and respect.

MASSACHUSETTS HOUSES MENTIONED OR PICTURED, BY TOWN

Town / Address	Figure No.	Page No.
Belmont		
200 Common Street	4.20, 4.35, 4.52	70, 78, 87
21 Stone Road	4.50	87
Beverly		
506 Hale Street	5.1	99
Boston		
Florian Island	5.5, 5.6	112, 112
90 Florian Street	5.7	113
30-50 Southbourne Road	5.8	114
80-82 Southbourne Road	5.9	115
84 Southbourne Road	5.10	115
296 Wachusett Street	5.5	112
Brewster		
2871 North Main Street	4.18, 4.41	69, 81
Brookline		
36 Amory Street	2.1	41
26 Beech Road	4.56, 4.56a	90
219 Buckminster Road	4.12, 4.54	65, 88
282 Buckminster Road	4.28	73
33 Circuit Road	4.45	84
42 Crafts Road	4.26	72

Town / Address	Figure No.	Page No.
59 Holland Road	4.6, 4.6a	59
227 Mason Terrace	4.48	86
55 Penniman Road	4.24	71
7 Pine Road	4.7	61
105 Rockwood Street	4.27	73
37 Salisbury Road	4.42	82
35 Spooner Road	4.38	79
61 Spooner Road	4.57	91
Cambridge		
16 Berkeley Street	4.46	84
202 Brattle Street	4.5	58
3 Clement Circle	4.36	79
11–15 Elmwood Avenue	4.39	80
36 Fresh Pond Parkway	4.17, 4.43	68, 82
117 Lake View Avenue	4.9, 4.40	65, 81
43 Reservoir Street	4.16	68
Concord		
345 Garfield Road	4.11, 4.34	65, 77
Easton		
359 Washington Street	5.3, 5.4	104, 105

Appendix B
MASSACHUSETTS HISTORICAL COMMISSION
INVENTORY FORMS, BY TOWN

Town	Address	Inventory No.	Author	Date
Arlington				
	35 Falmouth Road	50	Landscape Research	1980
	351 Mystic Street	95	Landscape Research	1980
Belmont				
	18 Blake Street	732	Judy Williams	1982
	15 Clover Street	450	Judy Williams	1982
	200 Common Street	48	Nora Luca	1982
	61 Stone Road	53	Nora Luca	1982
Beverly				
	506 Hale Street	493 and 934	M. Helper	1993
	Valley Road	697	M. Helper	1993
Boston				
Woodbourne				
	90 Florian Street	10540	no attribution	no date
	56–58 Southbourne	14469		
	60–70 Southbourne	14469		
	80 Southbourne	10554		
	84 Southbourne	10553		
	296 Wachusett	10545		

Town	Address	Inventory No.	Author	Date
Braintree				
	54 Cochato Street	252	Dempsey/Clemson	1999
Brewster				
	2871 Main Street	36	Donald E. Sackhein	1969
Brookline				
	36 Amory Street	64	R. C. S.	1977
	16 Beech Road	477	no attribution	1977
	26 Beech Road	476	Carla Benka	1983
	79 Buckminster Road	1984	Carla Benka	1983
	219 Buckminster Road	1573	Carla Benka	1983
	230 Buckminster Road	2000	Carla Benka	1983
	220 Buckminster Road	1999	Carla Benka	1983
	282 Buckminster Road	1491	Carla Benka	1980
	474 Chestnut Hill Avenue	1501	Leslie Larkin	1985
	33 Circuit Road	1569	Carla Benka	1983
	250 Clark Road	780	Carla Benka	1980
	189 Clinton Road			
	28 Copley Street	130	Carla Benka	1978
	43 Cottage Farm Road	81	Leslie Larkin	1980
	106 Crafts Road	2128	Carla Benka	1983
	41 Crafts Road	1552	Leslie Larkin	1980
	184 Dean Road	1499	Carla Benka	1980

Town	Address	Inventory No.	Author	Date
	77 Evans Road	373	Kapstein & Benka	1980
	50 Griggs Road	2597	Harwich, Benka, Reed	1985
	6–11 Griggs Terrace	2584	Harwich, Benka, Reed	1985
	40 Heath Hill Street	1286	Leslie Larkin	1983
	127 High Street	1159	Susan Dole	1976
	59 Holland Road	2064	Carla Benka	1983
	170 Ivy Street	41	R. C. S.	1977
	227 Mason Terrace	342	Carla Benka	1979
	55 Peniman Road	341	Carla Benka	1979
	7 Pine Road	1368	K. Wheeler/V. Benka	1979
	91 Seaver Street	1461	Benka, Lunham	1983
	35 Spooner Road	2171	Carla Benka	1983
	61 Spooner Road	2175	Carla Benka	1983
Cambridge				
	202 Brattle Street	81	John Swain	1976
	11–15 Elmwood Avenue	127	John Swain	1976
Cohasset				
	161 Atlantic Avenue	1160	David H. Wadsworth	1994
Concord				
	345 Garfield Street	296	Ann Forbes	1992
Dover				
	133 Claybrook Road	90	Emily Bertschy	1978

Town	Address	Inventory No.	Author	Date
Easton				
	359 Washington Street	40	Mrs. James Lee	1969
Gloucester				
	18–20 Eastern Point Boulevard	465	D. Hilbert, E. Woodford	1985
	13 Edgemoor Road	365	D. Hilbert, E. Woodford	1985
Lexington				
	6 Berwick	1033	Lisa Mausolf	2000
Dover				
	133 Farm Road	90	Emily Bertschy	1978
Longmeadow				
	41 Benedict Terrace	167	Kate Greenleese	1987
	25 Birchwood Street	1696	Kate Greenleese	1987
	39 Birchwood Street	1698	Kate Greenleese	1987
	55 Birchwood Street	1699	Kate Greenleese	1987
	100 Crescent Road	256	K. K. Kottoridis	1987
	1446 Longmeadow Street	1163	K. K. Kottoridis	1987
	21 Roseland Terrace	1780	K. K. Kottoridis	1987
	22 Park Avenue South	1800	Kate Greenleese	1987
	35 Woodlawn Place	1828	Kate Greenleese	1987
Milton				
	34 Century Lane	1852	Edith Clifford	2009
	118 Woodland Road	299	Edith Clifford	1986

Town	Address	Inventory No.	Author	Date
Newton				
	85 Bigelow Road	3868	Jenkins, Abele	1988
	1174 Boylston Street	5019	Gretchen G. Schuler	1983
	1547 Centre Street	3372	Jenkins, Abele	1988
	71 Chestnut Street	3872	Jenkins, Abele	1988
	652 Chestnut Street	4662		
	72 Dalton Street	2893	Jenkins, Abele	1988
	135 Essex Road	2679	Gretchen G. Schuler	1983
	15 Hobart Terrace	4512	Jenkins, Abele	1988
	14 Huntington Road	4472	Jenkins, Abele	1988
	150 Monadnock Road	4535	Jenkins, Abele	1987/88
	46 Suffolk Road	4650	Susan Abele	1989
	125 Windermere	6169	Umless, Rosenthal	2001
	47 Windsor Road	3822	Devorah Shea	1981
Northampton				
	98 Bancroft Road	358	Bonnie Parsons	2010
	230 North Main Street	55	Bonnie Parsons	2011
Salem				
	1–3 Orne Square	1065	Kim Withers Brengle	1995
	2–4 Orne Square	1063	Kim Withers Brengle	1995
	5–7 Orne Square	1066	Kim Withers Brengle	1995
	6–8 Orne Square	1062	Kim Withers Brengle	1995

Town	Address	Inventory No.	Author	Date
	9–11 Orne Square	1067	Kim Withers Brengle	1995
	10–12 Orne Square	1061	Kim Withers Brengle	1995
	14–16 Orne Square	1060	Kim Withers Brengle	1995
	15–17 Orne Square	1068	Kim Withers Brengle	1995
Springfield				
	141 Forest Park Avenue	2388	not available	not available
	208 Longhill Street	2107	not available	not available
	36 Maplewood Terrace	2284	not available	not available
	30 Oxford Street	2285	not available	not available
	51 Oxford Street	2324	not available	not available
	79 Riverview Terrace	2283	not available	not available
Watertown				
	173 Bellevue Road	136	Architectural Preservation Associates	1982
	93 Garfield Street	461	Architectural Preservation Associates	1982
Wellesley				
	9–11 Hampden Street	695	K. K. Boomer	1990
	12 Leighton Street	1351	K. K. Boomer/N. Rich	1990
	12 Weston Road	189	Sandra B. Carter	1980
	18 Whiting Road	1150		
Weston				
	23 Wellesley Street	338	Pamela W. Fox	1994

Town	Address	Inventory No.	Author	Date
Winchester				
	9 Calumet Road	43	Carol Ely	1979
	6 Everett Avenue	353	Carol Ely	1979
	17 Everett Avenue	681		
	32 Everett Avenue	364	Carol Ely	1979
	35 Everett Avenue	690		
	28 Lakeview Road	649		
	4 Lakeview Terrace	633		
	3 Sheffield West	372	Carol Ely	1979
Worcester				
	5 Montvale Road	1987	Shantia Anderheggen	1992

Sometimes it is necessary to use a technical word when describing architecture because it is the fastest and most accurate way to make one's point. I have tried to explain most of the technical words used in this work but not all of them. This glossary will make the meaning clear for those needing further elucidation.

⊰ A ⊱

arch: a curved symmetrical structure spanning an opening and typically supporting the weight of a bridge, roof, or wall above it.

gothic arch: a pointed arch, originally used in European and English cathedrals in the period between 1200 and 1500.
segmental arch: an arch whose curve is a circular arc of less than that of a half circle.
tudor arch: a wider, low elliptical or pointed arch, usually drawn from four centers.

ashlar: in masonry construction, a stone block with right-angled corners, laid in horizontal courses. Sometimes reproduced in wood to mimic stone.

⊰ B ⊱

balustrade: a row of small columns (balusters) topped by a rail. It is often found lining staircases and terraces.

banister: a handrail, usually on a staircase. Sometimes including its supporting structures.

bargeboard: a board, often ornately pierced or carved, attached along the projecting front edge a gable. Also called a *verge-board.* See also **raking cornice**.

battered: a slope on the outer face of a wall that recedes from bottom to top. A buttress is often battered.

belt course, also called a **string course**: a molding or projecting course running horizontally along the face of a building.

brackets: a device of wood, stone, or metal that projects from a wall to carry a weight such as a cornice.

buttress: a mass of masonry projecting from or built against a wall to give additional strength.

chimney shoulder: the sloped side of a masonry chimney where it changes from a wider width at its bottom to a narrower width for its vertical reach above the rooftop. Chimney shoulders are often covered in protective tile, slate, or brick.

corbelling: brick or masonry courses, each built out beyond the one below. Can be used as a support, although more frequently as a decorative device.

coursed, coursing: a horizontal row of brick or stone.

　random coursing: not laid in horizontal rows but randomly placed, often in seen in fieldstone walls or foundations.

cornice: aside from its use as the top projection of an entablature in classical architecture, the cornice describes the exterior trim located at the juncture of a wall and a roof.

　boxed cornice: it closes, by an enclosure, the distance between the eaves projecting beyond the building wall. Seen from below it resembles a box nestled against the building, sometimes highly decorated. Also described as a type of cornice with rafter ends covered by the fascia and soffit.

　open cornice: overhanging eaves with exposed rafters, visible from below, the ends of which are sometimes shaped to look like attractive brackets.

　raking cornice: a sloped timber on the outside-facing edge of a roof running between the ridge and the eave. A bargeboard is a raking cornice.

⊰ E ⊱

eave: the part of the roof that extends beyond the wall.

　eave return: the decorative extension of the eave that wraps around the gable end of the house. Sometimes called a cornice return.

⊰ F ⊱

façade: the principal front of a building.

facia: a horizontal piece (such as a board) covering the joint between the top of a wall and the projecting eaves.

⊰ G ⊱

gable: the vertical triangular end of a building from cornice or eaves to ridge; also the similar end of a gambrel roof.

　gable field: the triangular area outlined by a gable.

glass: bull's eye: a small, round piece, usually handblown with a visible center.

leaded glass: small panes of clear or stained glass held together with lead strips.

H

half-timbering: a method of construction in which the walls are made of large timbers and the spaces in-between are filled in with brick or plaster, or an imitation of this where the timbers are decoratively applied rather than structural.

hood: a protective or decorative cover over a door or window.

J

jerkin-head: see *roofs*

jetty (jettied): a building technique used in medieval timber-frame buildings in which an upper floor projects beyond the dimensions of the floor below to gain space on an upper floor and protect the wall beneath.

L

lath, lathing: wood or metal strips attached to framing members used to support an outer layer such as stucco, tile, or shingle.

lintel: a horizontal structural member that supports a load over an opening such as a door or window.

M

molding: a continuous decorative band of wood or masonry. Sometimes spelled **moulding.**

mullion: a large vertical member separating two or more windows.

muntin: A thin strip of wood or metal holding glass panes within a window.

P

pergola: a walkway in a garden featuring a double row of columns or pillars, usually covered by joists above. Often used in conjunction with vines trained on the columns.

piazza: no-longer-used word for a porch or terrace.

portico: a covered entry, or sometimes porch, supported by columns or pillars.

purlin: in a timber-framed roof, a horizontal member that runs between or on top of the rafters. Its ends may protrude beyond the roof.

⁂ Q ⁂

quoins: large rectangular stones, pieces of wood, or area of brick laid at the corners of a building to reinforce it or used as a decorative device to mimic a structural need. Often alternating large and small blocks.

⁂ R ⁂

rafter: in a timber-framed roof, a sloping member that supports the roof.

roofs: (see Chap 4)

    gable roof: having two pitches or slopes located either at the front (front gable) or side (side gable) of the building.
    pitched roof: a roof with two sloping sides.
    jerkin-head or clipped roof: a gable roof with a clipped or truncated gable.
    hip roof: a roof having four pitched sides.
    gambrel roof: a roof with a double slope on two sides of the building.
    catslide roof: a gable, gambrel, or hip roof with one pitch longer than the other and descending below the level of the other slope.

⁂ S ⁂

soffit: the underside of a cornice, arch, or box cornice.

string course: see **belt course.**

style:

    Gothic Revival Style: a Romantic, picturesque style, popular in America between 1840 and 1880, that adopted medieval design elements such as pointed arches and carved or filigree work on bargeboards and porches.
    Mission Revival Style: popular especially in the American West, but used elsewhere between 1890 and 1920. It sought inspiration in the architecture of the Spanish conquest. The Spanish Revival style, 1915–1940, introduced more elaborate forms and ornament from Spain and South American countries.
    Prairie Style: a midwestern style significant from 1900 to 1920 and an outgrowth of the English Arts and Crafts Movement.

Architect Frank Lloyd Wright and his peers introduced original, horizontally spread-out houses of great simplicity with carefully controlled ornamentation.

Queen Anne Style: extremely popular between 1880 and 1910, this style took many forms, but generally featured irregular roof shapes and massing, decorated porches, complicated wall and roof surfaces, and ornate decorative devices such as spindle-work, half-timbering, patterned brick, or shingle work.

T

terra cotta block: hollow block made from terra cotta, a clay product.

V

vernacular: non-architect-designed, folk, or preliterate architecture.

W

windows:

banked windows: groups of three or more windows closely spaced together in a horizontal plane.

bay window: a window set in a square or rectangular structure protruding from an exterior wall and supported by foundations or the ground.

bow window: a rounded bay window.

casement window: a window with the sash hinged at the side to open.

double-hung window: a window with two sashes that both usually rise and lower.

eyebrow window: a very low, arched dormer without sides.

oriel window: a roofed structure with a window protruding from an outside wall of a building, unsupported by foundations or the ground.

Adams, Tom. "The Indelible Mark of Addison LeBoutillier." The Andover Historical Society. http:andoverhistorical.org

American Institute of Architects. "Pioneers in Preservation: Biographical Sketches of Architects Prominent in the Field Before World War II." Washington, D. C., 1990.

Andrews, Robert. "The Changing Styles of Country Houses." *The Architectural Review*, January 1904.

The American Architect. "House of Winfield Smith, Esq. Brookline, E. B. Stratton, Architect." CIII (April 2, 1913).

——. "House of A. S. Warren, Esq. Northampton, Karl Scott Putnam, Architect." July 29, 1914.

The American Architect and Building News/The American Architect. "The Current Architectural Press." January 12, 1910.

——. "The Current Architectural Press." March 9, 1910.

——. House in Winchester (photograph). CV, no. 2000 (April 22, 1914).

——. House at 36 Amory Street, Brookline, Massachusetts. Plate 1688 (1908).

——. House at 189 Clinton Road Brookline, Massachusetts. February 1913.

——. House at 13 Berwick Street, Lexington, Massachusetts. January 1915.

——. House at 56 Garden Street Cambridge, Massachusetts. March 1924.

——. Tyler House, F. C. Brown, Architect, 33, (1913): 172–173

Architectural Record. House at 33 Circuit Road, Brookline, Massachusetts. XVI, 11 (November 1909): 151.

——. House at 13 Edgemoor Road, Gloucester, Massachusetts. XXIII (1908).

——. House at 359 Washington Street, Easton, Massachusetts. (July 1914).

Architectural Review, The. "Current Periodicals." 7, no. 4 (April 1900).

——. "Current Periodicals." 9, no. 11 (November 1902).

——. "Current Periodicals." 10, no. 2 (February 1903).

——. "Current Periodicals." 12, no. 5 (May 1903).

——. "Current Periodicals." 12, no. 6 (June 1903).

——. "Current Periodicals." 12, no. 12 (December 1905).

——. "Current Periodicals." 13, no. 1 (January 1906).

——. "Current Periodicals." 13, no. 6 (June 1906).

——. "Current Periodicals." 14, no. 12 (December 1907).

——. "Current Periodicals." 17, no. 2 (January 1910).

——. "Current Periodicals." 1, no. 4, (1912).

142 ———. "Current Periodicals." 3, no. 3 (1914).

———. "Publisher's Department." 13, no. III (February 1906).

———. "The House at 219 Buckminster Street Brookline, Massachusetts." (February 1913).

———. "House for Miss Cecilia Beaux." Plate XXXI and 8 photographs (February 1914).

———. "Modern English Design." 5, no. 4 (April 1917).

———. "Sunset Rock," House at 20 Eastern Point Boulevard, Gloucester, Massachusetts. Plate XXXI.

Ashbee, C. R. "Man and the Machine: The Soul of Architecture I." *The House Beautiful* VIII, no. 1 (1910).

———. "Man and the Machine: The Soul of Architecture II: Comparison Between English and American Architecture." *The House Beautiful* XXVIII, no. 2 (July 1910).

———. "Man and the Machine: Return to the Village: The Experiment of the Guild Handicraft." *The House Beautiful* XXVIII, no. 3 (August 1910).

———. "Man and the Machine: Return to the Village." *The House Beautiful* XXVIII, no. 4 (August 1910).

Aslet, Clive. *The Last Country Houses.* New Haven, CT: Yale University Press, 1982.

———. *The Arts and Crafts Country House: From the Archives of Country Life.* London: Aurum Press, 2011.

———. *The National Trust Building of the English House.* Hammondsworth, UK: Viking, 1985.

Baillie Scott, M. H. "A Country House." *The Studio* X, no. 37 (1900): 30–38.

———. *Houses and Gardens.* London: George Mewnes Ltd., 1906. https://archive.org/details/housesandgardenooscotgoog

Bairnsfather, Ragnhild M., ed. *Winchester, Massachusetts: The Architectural Heritage of a Victorian Town.* Winchester, Massachusetts: Winchester Historical Society, 1988.

Barnes, David I. "The Value of Stucco." *The House Beautiful*, June 1919.

Bein, Arthur G. "The House and Its Environment—Part I." *The American Architect*, January 5, 1910.

Boston Architectural Club. *Boston Architectural Club Year Book: Exhibition.* 1907.

———. *Year Book: Current Architecture.* 1916.

———. *Year Book: Current Architecture.* 1916: 11.

Boynton, Louis. "Planning the House and Garden." *House and Garden* 20 (November 1911).

Bragdon, Claud. "Plaster Houses." *The Architectural Review* XI, no. 1 (January 1904).

Brandt, Beverly K. "The Essential Link: Boston Architecture and the Society of Arts and Crafts, 1897–1917." Tiller, September–October 1983.

Brick and Clay Record. Building Brick Association of America Convention, "Proceedings in Full" (with illustrations of Woodbourne houses). XLII, no. 6 (March 15, 1913): 329–332.

———. "Forest Hills Community Built of Brick." 42, no. 6 (March 1914).

———. "Pittsburg, Pennsylvania." 44, no. 7 (April 7, 1914).

Brickbuilder, The. "Modern British Suburban Homes." 15, no. 2 (November 1906).

———. "Modern English Suburban Homes." 16, no. 1 (January 1907).

———. "Two Groups of Houses Built by the Boston Dwelling House Company, Kilham & Hopkins, Architects." 22, no. 4 (April 1913).

British Listed Buildings website: http://www.britishlistedbuildings.co.uk

25 Asmuns Hill

1–2 Eastholm

Brown, Frank Chouteau. "Suburban Homes." *Good Housekeeping* XXXVII, no. 4 (October 1903).

———. "The Relation Between English and American Domestic Architecture: The Influence of Materials." *The Brickbuilder* 15, no. 7 (July 1906).

———. "The Historical Derivation of Style." *The Brickbuilder* 15, no. 7 (July 1906).

———. "The Relation Between English and American Domestic Architecture: The Influence of Materials." *The Brickbuilder* 15, no. 8 (August 1906).

———. "The Relation Between English and American Domestic Architecture." *The Brickbuilder* 15, no. 9 (September 1906).

———. "The Relation Between English and American Domestic Architecture: Modern English Work." *The Brickbuilder* 15, no. 10 (October 1906).

———. "Exterior Plaster Construction." *The Architectural Review* 14, no. 1 (January 1907).

———. "Boson Suburban Architecture." *The Architectural Review,* April 1907.

———. "Fire-proof Dwelling Interiors." *The Architectural Review* 17, no. 3 (March 1910).

———. "The Small Country House." *The Architectural Record* 28, no. 3 (September 1910).

———. "The Use and Abuse of Half-Timber Work." *The House Beautiful* 34, no. 5 (October 1913).

———. "Natco Tile—Its Development in House Building." *The Natco Double House—Semi-detached, Attractive, Economical, Durable.* Pittsburg: National Fire Proofing Co., and Boston: Rogers and Mason, 1914.

———. "Workingmen's Housing at Hopedale, Mass." *The Architectural Review* 21, no. 4 (April 1916).

———. "Gidea Park: A Typical English Garden City." *The Architectural Review* 5 (April 1917).

Bunting, Bainbridge, and Robert H. Nylander. *Report Four: Old Cambridge.* Cambridge, MA: Cambridge Historical Commission, MIT Press, 1973.

Candee, Richard M. and Greer Hardwicke. "Early Twentieth-Century Reform Housing by Kilham & Hopkins, Architects of Boston." *Winterthur Portfolio* 22, no. 1 (Spring 1987). http://www.jstor.org/stable/1181147

Chapin, F. Stewart. "Immigration as a Source of Urban Increase." *American Statistical Association* 14, no. 107 (September 1914). http://www.jstor.org/stable/2964952

Chapman and Frazer. *Architectural Achievements: Chapman and Frazer, Architects.* Boston: J. Hewitt, 1925.

144 Cook, Fredrick, and William Grundy. *The Population of Massachusetts as Determined by the Fourteenth Census of the United States—1920.* Boston: Wright and Potter, 1921. http://babel.hathitrust.org/

Country Life in America (Clinton Wire Cloth advertisement). XXXI, no. 1 (November 1916): 64.

Crawford, Margaret. *Building the Workingman's Paradise: The Design of American Company Towns.* London: Verso, 1995.

Croly, Herbert. "The Work of Kilham & Hopkins." *The Architectural Record*, XXI, no. 2 (February 1912).

Cumming, Elizabeth, and Wendy Kaplan. *The Arts and Crafts Movement.* London: Thames & Hudson, 2002.

Cunningham, Mary P. "A Small House Which Revels in Flowers." *The House Beautiful*, XLVIII, no. V (November 1920): 387.

Davy, Peter. *Arts and Crafts Architecture.* London: Phaidon, 1995.

_____ . *Arts and Crafts Architecture: The Search for Earthly Paradise.* London: The Architectural Press, 1980.

_____ . *L'Architecture Arts & Crafts.* Bruxelles: Mardaga, 1987.

Dawnber, E. Guy. "The Home from the Outside" in Sparrow, W. Shaw, ed. *The British Home of Today: A Book of Modern Domestic Architecture and the Applied Arts.* New York: A. C. Armstrong and Son. 1904.

Duell, Mark, "Stunning Mansion Built by Architect Sir Edwin Lutyens Boasts Nine Bedrooms. . . ." *Daily Mail.* July 8, 2013.

Elder-Duncan, J. H. *Country Cottages and Weekend Homes.* New York: 1907.

Elzner, A. O. "The Artistic Expression of Concrete." *The American Architect* XCIII, no. 1676 (February 5, 1908).

Embury, Aymar, II. *One Hundred Country Houses: Modern American Examples.* New York: Century Co., 1909.

_____ . *The Livable House.* New York: Moffat Yard, 1917.

Fishman, Robert. *Urban Utopias in the Twentieth Century: Ebenezer Howard, Frank Lloyd Wright, Le Corbusier.* Cambridge: MIT Press, 1982.

Floyd, Margaret Henderson. *Architecture After Richardson: Regionalism Before Modernism—Longfellow, Alden and Harlow in Boston and Pittsburgh.* Chicago: University of Chicago Press, 1994.

Frampton, Kenneth. *Modern Architecture: A Critical History.* 4th ed. London: Thames and Hudson, 2007.

Freethy, W. J. "A Seashore House of Unusual Design." *Keith's Magazine* XXIV, no. 1 (January 1913).

Friedman, Donald. *Historical Building Construction: Design, Materials, Technology.* New York: W. W. Norton, 2010.

G. "The Revival of English Domestic Architecture VI: The Work of Mr. C. F. A. Voysey." *The International Studio.* July 1897.

Griffin, Kathryn. "History of a Grand Cape Cod Estate." *Cape Cod Compass.* Greensted, Mary. *The Arts and Crafts Movement in Britain.* Oxford, UK: Shire Publications, 2011.

Gregory, Edward W. "Some English Country Houses." *The House Beautiful* XXIX (May 1911).

_____ . "Architects of the Modern English Home: 1. The Work of Mr. M. H. Baillie Scott." *The House Beautiful*, August 1911.

_____ . "Architects of the Modern English Home: 2, The Work of R. Barry Parker." *The House Beautiful*, XXX, no. 4 (September 1911).

_____ . "Garden Cities of England." *The House Beautiful*, May 1912.

Grimmer, Anne E. "The Preservation and Repair of Historic Stucco." *Preservation Brief #22*, NPS Technical Preservation Services, Washington, D. C.

Haigh, Diane. *Baillie Scott: The Artistic House*. London: Academy Editions, 1995.

"H. C. Frick's Party Draws Thousands." *New York Times*, August 17, 1912.

Heath, Richard. "Woodbourne and the Boston 1915 Movement." Jamaica Plain (MA) Historical Society.

Hering, Oswald C. *Concrete Homes: The Use of Plastic Materials in the Building of Country and Suburban Houses*. New York: The Country House Library, McBride, Nast & Co., 1912. Also, Robert M. McBride & Co., 1922, revised edition.

Hewitt, Alan. *The Architect and the American Country House*, New Haven, CT: Yale University Press, 1990.

Hitchmough, Wendy. *CFA Voysey*. London: Phaidon Press, 1995.

Holme, Charles. "Modern British Domestic Architecture and Decoration." *The Studio*, Special Summer edition, 1901.

——— . "Country Houses." *The House Beautiful* 25, no. 1 (May 1909).

——— . "The Residence of E. J. Alsop, Esq. at Milton, Massachusetts, Chapman and Frazer, Architects." *House and Garden*, December 1920.

Howe, Lois Lily. "Serving Pantries in Small Suburban Houses." *The Architectural Review* XIV, no. 3 (March 1907).

Howes, Benjamin A. "The Use of Concrete in the Building of the Small Country House." *American Homes and Gardens*, April 1909.

Hyde, Matthew, and Esmé Whittaker. *Arts and Crafts Houses in the Lake District*. London: Frances Lincoln Limited, 2014.

Jackson, Allen W. "The Case for the Half-Timber House." *House and Garden* 17, no. 10 (January 1910).

——— . *The Half-Timbered House*. New York: McBride, Nast & Co., 1912.

——— . "Homes that Architects Have Built for Themselves." *House and Garden* XXIV, no. 5 (November 1913).

Jackson, Kenneth. *Crabgrass Frontier: The Suburbanization of the United States*. New York: Oxford University Press, 1985.

Kilham & Hopkins. "The Houses for the Salem Rebuilding Trust." *The Architectural Review* 21, no. 4 (April 1916).

——— . "House in Dorchester, Massachusetts." *The Architectural Review* XIV, no. 3 (March 1907).

Kimball, Richard Boland. "An Example of Creative Building." *The House Beautiful* XLVIII, no. V (November 1920): 376.

Kimmel, Michael S. "Review of Three Books." *Contemporary Sociology* 16, no. 3 (May 1987).

Kornwolf, James D. *M. H. Baillie Scott and the Arts and Crafts Movement*. Baltimore, MD, & London: The Johns Hopkins Press, 1972.

Little, J. Lovell, Jr. "A $5,000 House for a Family of Four." *Indoors and Out*, January 1906.

——— . "Exterior Plaster as a Substitute for Wood." *The Architectural Review* 13, no. 4 (April 1906).

——— . "A Suburban House." *The House Beautiful*, November 1906.

——— . "House at Chestnut Hill, Massachusetts." *The Architectural Review* XIV, no. 3 (March 1907). Illustrates 33 Circuit Road Brookline, Massachusetts.

——— . "Three Plaster Houses: J. Lovell Little." (House at Chestnut Hill, from the street), *The Architectural Review* 16, no. 11 (November 1909).

——— . "Modern English Plaster Houses for America." *House and Garden*, March 1910.

146 ____. "The English Plaster House" in Saylor, Henry, ed. *Architectural Styles for Country Houses: The Characteristics and Merits of Various Types of Architecture as Set Forth by Enthusiastic Advocates.* New York: McBride, Nast & Co., 1912.

____. "A Charming Small Suburban House of Cement." *The House Beautiful* (June 1919): 356.

"Little Thakeham." *Indoors and Out* 1, no. 1 (1907).

Lynch, Gerald. "Tudor Brickwork." Cathedral Communications Ltd., 2012.

Massey, James C., and Shirley Massey. "English Arts and Crafts Houses in America." *Old House Journal,* January/February 2005.

McAlester, Virginia Savage, and Lee McAlester. *A Field Guide to American Houses.* New York: Alfred A. Knopf, 1986.

McAlester, Virginia Savage. *A Field Guide to American Houses.* New York: Alfred A Knopf. 2013.

Meacham, Standish. *Regaining Paradise: Englishness and the Early Garden City Movement.* New Haven: Yale University Press, 1999.

Meister, Maureen. *Architecture and the Arts and Crafts Movement in Boston: Harvard's H. Langford Warren.* Lebanon, NH: University Press of New England, 2003.

____. *Arts and Crafts Architecture: History and Heritage in New England.* Hanover, NH: University Press of New England, 2014.

Migeon, Jaques. "Red House and Ruskin." *Journal of the William Morris Society,* Spring, 1977, pp. 30-32.

Miller, Mervyn. *English Garden Cities.* Swindon, UK: English Heritage, 2010.

Murphy, Edgar Gardner. *Child Labor in Alabama: An Appeal to the People and Press of New England with a Resulting Correspondence. Letters from Mr. J. Howard Nicholas and Mr. Horace S. Sears.* Montgomery, AL: Montgomery Child Labor Committee, 1901.

Muthesius, Hermann. *The English House.* Edited by Dennis Sharp. New York: Rizzoli, 1987.

Nichols, Rose Standish. "Local Color in Architecture." *The House Beautiful* 29, no. 3 (February 1911).

Northend, Mary Harrod. "The Interesting Stucco House of W. C. Strong, Esq., at Waban, Massachusetts." *American Homes and Gardens,* October 1909.

____. "A House at Newton, Massachusetts." *American Homes and Gardens* (December 1912): 428.

O'Connell, James C. *The Hub's Metropolis: Greater Boston's Development from Railroad Suburb to Smart Growth.* Cambridge, MA: MIT Press, 2013.

O'Gorman, James F., ed. *Drawing Towards Home.* Boston: Historic New England, 2010.

O'Neill, Daniel. *Lutyens: Country Houses.* London: Lund Humphries Publishers Ltd., 1980.

Outka, Elizabeth. *Consuming Traditions: Modernity, Modernism, and the Commodified Authentic. . . .* Oxford, UK: Oxford University Press, 2008.

Parker, Barry. "Beauty in Buildings and Some Things that Lead to It." *The Craftsman,* June 1902.

Parker, Barry. "Modern Country Homes in England: Number Three." *The Craftsman,* 18, no. 3 (June 1910).

Parker, Barry, and Raymond Unwin. *The Art of Building a Home: A Collection of Lectures and Illustrations.* London: Longmans, Green and Co., Mayfield Press, 1901.

Price, William L. "Model Houses: A $3500 to $4000 Suburban House." In *Home Building and Furnishing*, William L. Price and William Martin Johnson. New York: Doubleday, Page and Co., 1903.

Prior, Edward S. "The Moment of English Architecture." *The Architectural Review*, 10, no. 2 (February 1903).

Retig, Robert Bell. *Guide to Cambridge Architecture: Ten Walking Tours*. Cambridge, MA: MIT Press, 1969.

Rowe, Peter, and Alexander Von Hoffman. "Woodbourne: An Early Garden City Experiment in Affordable Living." *Form, Modernism and History*. Essays in Honor of Eduard F. Sekler. Harvard University Graduate School of Design/Harvard University Press. 1997.

Royal Institute of British Architects. "The Small Country House: A Collection of Inexpensive But Well Designed Suburban Dwellings." *Journal of the Royal Institute of British Architects* 28 (July–December 1910): 282.

Royal Institute of British Architects. *English Arts and Crafts Movement: A Book of Postcards*. Petaluma, California: Pomegranate Communications, Inc., RIBA British Architectural Library, 2008.

Ruskin, John. *The Lamp of Beauty*. Edited by Joan Evans. London: Phaidon Press Ltd., 1959, 1995.

_____. *The Stones of Venice*. Edited by Jan Morris. Boston: Little, Brown & Co. 1981.

Salmon, Lucy M. "The Garden City Cheap Cottages Exhibition." *The Craftsman* IX, no. 2 (November 1905).

Saylor, Henry, ed. *Architectural Styles for Country Houses: The Characteristics and Merits of Various Types of Architecture as Set Forth by Enthusiastic Advocates*. New York: McBride, Nast & Co., 1912.

Shermerhorn, C. E. "The Modern Kitchen and Its Planning." *House & Garden* XXIV, no. 5 (November 1913).

Simpson, Duncan. *C. F. A. Voysey: An Architect of Individuality*. London: Lund Humphries Publishers Ltd., 1979.

Simpson, Pamela H. *Cheap, Quick and Easy: Imitative Architectural Materials, 1870–1930*. Knoxville, TN: University of Tennessee Press, 1999.

Spencer, Ellen. "Robert Coit: Houses and Public Buildings in an Age of Suburban Growth.", *The Architects of Winchester, Massachusetts*, no. 8, Winchester, MA: Winchester Historical Society (2007).

Spenser, Robert C., Jr. "The Work of Frank Lloyd Wright." *The Architectural Review* 7, no. 5 (May 1900).

_____. "Of What Shall the House Be Built: The Advantage of Roughcast" *Indoors and Out* 2, no. 4 (1906).

_____. "Casements." *The House Beautiful* XXIV, no. 2 (July 1908): 44.

Spiers, John H. "Landscaping the Garden City: Transportation, Utilities, and Parks in Newton, Massachusetts 1874 to 1915."

Stickley, Gustav. *Craftsman Homes*. New Jersey: Random House, Gramercy Books, 1995. Originally published in 1909.

_____. *More Craftsman Homes*, New York: The Craftsman Publishing Co., 1912.

Swank, James M., "The Manufacture of Iron in New England" in Davis, William T., *The New England States: The Constitutional, Judicial, Educational, Commercial, Professional and Industrial History Vol. 1*, Boston: D. H. Hurd, 1897.

Swift, Samuel, "Garden City I: A Humanitarian Project Now Being Realized in England." *Indoors and Out* 1, no. 1 (October 1905).

148

Tinniswood, Adrian. *The Arts and Crafts House*. New York: Watson-Guptill Publications, 1999.

Todd, Pamela. *The Arts and Crafts Companion*. London: Thames & Hudson, 2008.

Town of Weston. "Wellesley Street Area Historical Narrative." Unsigned, undated. http://www.weston.org/

Town of Weston. "Pigeon Hill Area Historical Narrative." Unsigned, undated. http://www.weston.org

Turner, James. *The Liberal Education of Charles Eliot Norton*. Baltimore, MD: Johns Hopkins Press, 1999.

Varella, Hazel L.

Easton, (MA), Historical Society, Historical Images of Easton on Flickr, "Hafstrom-Swanson House, aka Twin Cottages." https://www.flickr.com/photos/historicalimagesofeastonma/22283821736/in/photostream/

Easton, (MA), Historical Society, Historical Images of Easton on Flickr, "Main Street, Ames, Oliver, 267 Main Street, North Easton, Massachusetts, built in 1893, razed in 1946, Sheep Pasture" https://www.flickr.com/photos/historicalimagesofeastonma/15367049074

Voysey, C. F. A. "Remarks on Domestic Entrance Halls." *The Studio* XI.

_____. *Individuality*. London: Chapman and Hall Ltd., 1915.

Wallick, Ekin. *The Small House for a Moderate Income*. New York: Hearst's International Library Co., Inc., 1915.

Warner, Jack. "Voysey's Buildings and the Arts and Crafts Movement." The C. F. A. Society. www.voysey/biography/architecture.html

Warren, H. Langston, "Recent Domestic Architecture in England." *The Architectural Review* 11, no. 1 (January 1904).

Weaver, Sir Lawrence. *Small Country Houses of To-day, Vol. I*. London: *Country Life*, and New York: Scribners, 3rd edition, 1922.

Wescott, John. "The Newtons II: Mature American Suburbs." *Indoors and Out* 1, no. 2 (1905).

Whipple, Harvey, and C. D. Gilbert. "Concrete Houses." *Concrete* 12, no. 1 (January 1918).

White, Charles E., Jr. "The Landscape Architect and the House." *The House Beautiful* XXXI, no. 4 (March 1912).

_____. "The Best Way to Use Cement." *The House Beautiful* 34, no. 5 (October 1913).

_____. "W. H. Bidlake and His Recent Work." *House & Garden* 4, no. 4 (October 1903).

Winter, Robert, and Alexander Vertikoff. *Craftsman Style*. New York: Harry N. Abrams, Inc., 2004.

Withey, Henry F., and Elsie Rathburn Withey. *Biographical Dictionary of American Architects (Deceased)*. Los Angeles: New Age Publishing, 1956.

Wood, Esther. "Some Modern Cottages." *The Studio* 22 (March 1901).

Wright, Frank Lloyd. "The Art and Craft of the Machine." *Brush and Pencil* 8, no. 2 (May 1901).

Wright, Peter B. "Fireproof Suburban Houses." *The House Beautiful* 25, no. 6 (May 1909).

Yorke, Trevor. *Arts and Crafts House Styles*. Newbury, UK: Countryside Books, 2011.

Zimerman, M. K., "Pittsburg, PA." *Brick and Clay Record* 44, no. 7 (April 7, 1914): 843.

CREDITS

All photographs not listed are by the author.

❧ Chapter 1 ❧

Figure 1.1. Red House, Bexleyheath, London. Photograph by Margery Wunch.

Figure 1.2. Perrycroft, Colwell, Northumberland. Photograph by Jessica Meltsner.

Figure 1.3. The Orchard, Chorley Wood, Hertfordshire. Photograph from Angus Trumble.

Figure 1.5. Munstead Wood, Godalming, Surrey. Courtesy of *Country Life*.

❧ Chapter 2 ❧

Figure 2.2b. 47 Windsor Street, Newton. From "The Interesting Stucco House of W. C. Strong, Esq., at Waban, Massachusetts" by Mary Harrod Northend in *American Homes and Gardens*, October 1909.

❧ Chapter 4 ❧

Figure 4.1. Clinton Wire Lath Co. advertisement from *Country Life in America*, XXXI, no. 1 (November 1916): 64.

Figure 4.8. Plan, 42 Waterston Road, Newton. From "A House at Newton, Massachusetts" by Mary Harrod Northend, *American Homes and Gardens* (December 1912): 428.

Figure 4.14. 76–78 Endicott Street, Salem. Photograph by Pamela Hartford.

Figure 4.26. 41 Crafts Road, Brookline. From "A Small House Which Revels in Flowers" by Mary P. Cunningham in *The House Beautiful*, XLVIII, V (November 1920): 387.

Figure 4.33. Advertisement for casement window hardware in *The House Beautiful* (November 1908): iv.

Figure 4.36. 3 Clement Circle, Cambridge. "Home of Professor B. L. Robinson, Cambridge, Massachusetts" in *The Architectural Review*, XII, no. 6 (June 1905): 150.

Figure 4.44. Advertisement for Pearl brand screens in *The House Beautiful* (June 1919): 378.

ACKNOWLEDGMENTS

My thanks go out to the people who helped me, most importantly my husband Michael Meltsner, my first reader, peerless editor, and unstinting booster whose all-inclusive support included two research trips to England: grateful doesn't begin to be an adequate expression. Included in those for whom I am particularly thankful are Jessica Meltsner, Brian Britt, Lucy and Anna Britt and Molly Meltsner, Ken Troop, and Will and Tessa Troop. Their patience, forbearance, and teasing have been sustaining.

Crucial to this endeavor were Bonnie Parsons, who has always been there, and Marjory Wunsch, who undertook critical research and photography in England: both were readers as well. Pamela Hartford, Barbara Graham, and Susan Maycock also accepted the laborious and time-consuming job of reading the manuscript—they are abundantly thanked here. Robert Bell Retig and Michael Steinitz extended their early encouragement; Peter Cresswell and Angus Trumble allowed me to use their photographs, and Anthony Zannino helped with technical problems.

Part of the pleasure of this book was the generous attention of the archivists at the Letchworth Study Center, Garden City Collection—Aimee Flack, Collections Officer, and her staff. Lynne Cumming, Deputy Manager, Letchworth Garden City Tourist Information Centre helped me plan my day in Letchworth. My daughter Jessica Meltsner not only accompanied me to visit Voysey's Perrycroft but took the photo of it that appears in Chapter 1. Gillian Archer, Perrycroft's owner, graciously showed us Perrycroft's marvelous interior and allowed our family to wander its exquisite formal gardens.

Thanks to the hardworking people at Bauhan Publishers: Sarah Bauhan, Henry James, and Mary Ann Faughnan. They have immeasurably improved the book, for which I am very grateful.

In Massachusetts, all the people noted below went out of their way to give me help, information, or access to their houses, and in some cases, historic documents or photographs. I could not have written this book without them.

Belmont
Sandra Rosenblum
Roy Epstein
Beverly
Marian Clarke
Boston
Earl Taylor, Dorchester Historical Society

Braintree
Donna Willoughby
Brookline
Spring Salavin
Laure Patton
Alan Morse

Cambridge
Jane Epstein
Louisa McCall
Jan Ferarra
Cohasset
Dick Tosi
Concord
Jon Jenkins
Dorchester
Earl Taylor, Dorchester Historical Society
Dover
Elisha Lee
Easton
Frank Meninno, Easton Historical Society and Museum
Nicole B. Casper, Archives and Historical Collections, Stonehill College
Gloucester
Lois Hamilton
Lexington
Lester and Cindy Savage
Manchester by the Sea
Christine Virden, Manchester by the Sea Historical Society

Milton
Chris Piatt
Newton
Sara Goldberg Historic Newton
Katy Hax Holmes
Neva Hax
John Dias
North Andover
Inga Larson
Rockport
Gwendolyn Stephenson
Salem
Pamela Hartford
Weston
Henry Reeder
Susan Wayne
Winchester
Giovanni Abbadessa
Worcester
Susan Ceccacci